GOOD ENOUGH?

GOOD ENOUGH?

Chris Cowdrey
and Jonathan Smith

Pelham Books

First published in Great Britain by
Pelham Books Ltd
44 Bedford Square
London WC1B 3DP
1986

British Library Cataloguing in Publication Data

Cowdrey, Chris
   Good enough?
   1. Cricket—England
   I. Title   II. Smith, Jonathan
   796.35'8'0924   GV919

ISBN 0 7207 1675 6

Printed and bound in Great Britain
by Butler & Tanner Ltd, Frome and London

Contents

1 Son of . . . 1

2 From Colchester to Calcutta? 18

3 Lord's Final: the greatest ever? 28

4 India: out of the shadow? 52
   (i)   A week in Bombay. My first Test Match
   (ii) Delhi, Second Test
   (iii) India from England: Jonathan Smith
   (iv) Madras, the perfect Test
   (v)   India: the press
   (vi) India? An impression

5 In the spotlight? Australia 93
   (i)   0 in Melbourne
   (ii) Listening to Larwood
   (iii) Australia: Jonathan Smith

6 1985 107
   (i)   Captain of Kent
   (ii) Richard Ellison
   (iii) Paul Downton
   (iv) Caught Knott bowled Underwood
   (v)   Bowling to Botham
   (vi) Kent in 1985: Jonathan Smith

7 On tour 156

8 Flashback 183

Quite often in recent years I have written down my thoughts and feelings on cricket: perhaps a few pages while in a hotel, or a thousand-word article for a magazine, or a tour reflection on a player. I hoped all this might one day build into a book. But a professional travels and plays, plays and travels, and I somehow didn't get it organised.

Then Jonathan Smith told me he also was thinking over a cricket book, in his case a novel. We spent hours going into my reactions to everything, analysing my views and by the time we'd finished we had agreed to write one together. The idea excited both of us. After all, we've known each other for fifteen years and with my ten years as a player and his experience with novels and drama it promised to be an interesting collaboration.

Because I want to make it clear that this is a collaboration not a ghost-written book. I have said what I wanted to say. So has Jonathan. He has chipped in with comments on an issue and observations on a game or tour in which I've been involved. We have talked together after matches, sent each other tapes, but written separately. Sometimes we have disagreed.

I hope you will enjoy my view from the middle or the dressing room, and I hope you enjoy his from the stand or the writer's desk. *Good Enough?* is a partnership between a cricketer who loves to write and a writer who loves cricket.

Chris Cowdrey

1

Son of . . .

I was only nine when I was selected for the 1st XI at my prep school, Wellesley House in Broadstairs. The others in the team were twelve- or thirteen-year-old boys in their final term. I remember this first game (against Tormore School) for it was the biggest occasion of my life, a Lord's final, with all the dreams and build-up and expectation, not to mention the extra buzz when a nine-year-old Cowdrey was included.

Extremely nervous and totally overawed, I easily ran out our best two players and made only seven. Seven. Innings finished and only seven. As soon as I was out I longed to field, to redeem myself, and when I did I had a simple chance of a run out but, in the excitement of contributing something to the game at last, I hurled it as hard as I could at the bowler, nearly breaking his hand. The chance of glory was gone. There was no other. (I thought the bowler should have been behind the stumps, allowing the chance of a direct hit, but I didn't dare say anything.)

Near the end of the day I did hold a high catch, which helped a little to lift the gloom and despondency of my big match debut, my big match failure. My grandfather, Stuart Chiesman, had come to watch me. It was clear he had not been impressed. However with great generosity he turned to me before leaving and said: 'That was a very good catch, Christopher.'

That makes me smile now, the sound of someone searching for something to praise in an otherwise bad performance. I wonder what he would have said if I had dropped it.

When we arrived back at Wellesley there was a bigger buzz around the corridors and under the trees. 'How many did

Cowdrey get?' 'Did Cowdrey get 50?' 'He ran out the captain!' 'Did he bowl?' 'No.' 'Only seven runs?' 'Yes, only seven.'

Later that evening I began to feel the full force of the day's disappointments in the middle. I had failed, and failure is the cricketer's most common experience, but I wasn't used to it.... Even in those early years I had already played a fair bit of most sports, and being bigger than many of my age group I tended to dominate. With this background of success, a success based on the advantage of early opportunity, I found my day trip to Tormore particularly upsetting. I cried in bed, wishing the big game was to be coming up tomorrow not gone today. But there was also that strange feeling of relief, relief that I wouldn't have to go through that pressure again. Failure, yes, but release from pressure, the two emotions I was to know so well.

Pressure ... pressure ... For the first time I became aware of being under the spotlight, son of Colin (I was baptised by the Rev David Sheppard, a former England captain and now Bishop of Liverpool, and my godfathers were Peter Richardson and Peter May, now chairman of selectors. Perhaps by those very choices I had already been 'selected' for attention.)

Any other child, aged nine, would have travelled for that small boys' game, failed miserably as well, but probably little would have been expected of him. On his return he would have slipped quietly back into the school routine, tea at 6.30, bath at 7.30, lights out 8.30.

'Oh, by the way, how did you get on today? ... Bad luck ... Never mind! What's Tormore like? Is it as nice as Wellesley?'

That might have been the sum of it.

If you push someone forward as a sportsman or as an academic he can very easily, whatever his gifts and effort, lose contact with the rest of his year. His 'promotion' can provoke easy and considerable resentment, not to mention envy. A clever schoolfriend of mine was placed in a class well ahead of his age group. Intellectually the decision was right, probably a necessity, but we all thought (and said) he was getting special treatment. 'Who the hell does he think he is?' Our jealousy cost him many friends and led him to arrogance. Both our behaviour to him and his to us contributed to the eventual problem.

This was my danger, aged nine, playing cricket with the senior members of the school, including the head boy. I would like to think I didn't become arrogant, but I was regularly put into detention for being 'bumptious'. What *did* 'bumptious' mean? I never knew and felt it tactful not to ask.

Sitting throughout the morning in a class (for those with limited ability) and playing cricket all afternoon with older boys was a problem, a problem intensified in my case because people were excessively interested in my progress in the game. When I went to the wicket groups would gather round the boundary because Colin Cowdrey was captain of England; indeed the 'old man' was scoring a hundred for England in his hundredth Test match, and this was the eldest son at the wicket.

'How is young Christopher progressing?'

I had no plans to play cricket as a career, so even at that age I tried to shrug off the comparison and scrutiny, looking forward more to soccer, because I was going to play for Chelsea when I grew up. Peter Osgood, John Hollins ... Chris Cowdrey ... My father hadn't played soccer for Chelsea and England, had he?

As I moved to Tonbridge School at the age of 13, the pros and cons of having a famous father became more obvious. In some ways people had already regarded me as a bit of a celebrity, and this had the joint effect of bringing me many friends without ever quite knowing who were the genuine ones. Sometimes I went out to tea with a boy's parents, never quite sure who had invited me, the boy or the parent. After a year or so at Tonbridge this 'friendship', the desire to be associated with famous people, had fortunately diminished.

In my second summer term, aged 14, I was selected for the 1st XI in the opening game. This re-run of my prep school experience had similar implications, although the comparisons being made now were more serious. With a professional's career beginning at 17 or 18 there were some people already predicting a future England player ('But he'll never be as good as his father').

Accepting the congratulations on my Tonbridge 1st XI selection I had mixed feelings. Still the same build-up and expectation and dreams (that never changes, whatever your age) but I was now asking myself:

'Am I that good? Can it be, both at Wellesley and Tonbridge, that I *had* to be promoted so early in my career? Would I have been selected if my name wasn't Cowdrey? If my name was Smith?'

In case I'd missed the point a few people made it to my face. Others hoped I would do well to shut the mutterers up ('Silence the critics', that famous press-box cliché). And just to remind me that my achievement wasn't really all that outstanding:

'His father was picked for Tonbridge 1st XI when he was only thirteen.'

Yet again I played alongside schoolboys four years older than myself, including (again) the head boy. Again I failed miserably. Opening the batting I was out in the first over or two for 0. That sinking feeling again, that feeling as before – so much was expected of me and I had allowed the nerves to get through. Would it have been better not to play?

It took several weeks before I scored a half-century, in an away match at Wellington College. Mike Bushby, the cricket master, was obviously delighted; and Ray Dovey, the former Kent player and Tonbridge professional said: 'I'm very pleased, Chris. It hasn't been easy for you, has it?'

Leaving the ground I was told by a member of the team that I would have been dropped for the game if my father hadn't invited everyone to stop off for a meal on our return journey! I was unable to handle that remark.

I ended up having a good season, and fully aware of the problem of having a famous father. I was beginning to sense what to expect should I ever be 'good enough' to play first-class cricket. The advantage of being his son was of course the 'recognition', the coverage and attention I received, yet the inevitable comparisons sometimes made me feel I was running with a following breeze into a head wind.

I thoroughly enjoyed my cricket at Tonbridge – good wickets, good coaching, good fixtures – yet I dreaded dad coming to watch. Often I failed in his presence. He usually hid behind a tree so that I wouldn't spot him, but he was such a big talking point, a famous player on the ground, I was soon told where he was:

'There's your father.'

'Where?'

'Over there.'

'Oh, yes.'

Captain of Tonbridge School 1st XI. Richard Ellison is on the extreme left of the picture and Nick Kemp, who played for Kent and Middlesex, is on my left (*Kent & Sussex Courier*)

Snick.

I always found it embarrassing. I expect he did too.

In 1974 I was picked for Young England against the West Indies at Lord's. At sixteen I was the youngest player in the side, the selection prompting exactly the same doubts in my mind: should someone from Yorkshire or Gloucestershire be playing instead, someone no one had heard of, a good player with an unknown name? Am I really, at 16, one of the best eleven under-19 players in England? But if I could see that I had been selected for the wrong reason it would lead to a loss of confidence, to the feeling the eyes on the boundary were willing me to fail. Fortunately the first ball I received was a very fast full toss on leg stump from a young Wayne Daniel. I dropped my bat on it, it flew to the leg-side boundary. Heads in the crowd nodded, 'He can play a bit, this boy.' (The next full toss from Wayne Daniel came a decade later, on the same ground, in the Nat West Final. Caught Radley, bowled Daniel.)

In 1976 the stakes were higher still: this time I was appointed captain of Young England to tour the Caribbean, and the side I was leading was a fine one. In case you think I'm exaggerating, it included Gower, Gatting, Gould, Athey, Allott and Downton! I may have been successful as a player and captain at school but I was aware of some resentment among the players at the sight of the skipper, 'young Cowdrey'. There's often a hint of that in all teams when they see who is appointed captain, and it usually doesn't last long. Anyway it was a feeling I anticipated and could well understand. Here was a public schoolboy (which can cause blood pressure to rise in some cricket circles) with a famous name (well, that's why he's in the side) and the extra suspicion that the main value of a Cowdrey would be to encourage the sponsors and add a bit of kudos.

An unbeaten trip helped me overcome self-doubts.

My debut for Kent was not in the championship. As one or two leading players were being rested I was thrown in against the Australians at Canterbury. Delighted as I was, the thought of batting at Canterbury in front of a full house, against the Aussies, brought predictable thoughts, thoughts well established since Wellesley and Tonbridge. In a corresponding fixture two years previously my father had played one of his very finest innings. Having set Kent 354 to win on the final day Ian Chappell was so sure of an Aussie victory he had booked the team coach for 3.30 in the afternoon. At 6.15 they left the ground well beaten: Colin Cowdrey 151 not out.

Many, many people reminded me of these details before I took the field at Canterbury, and with the weather bad, the wicket wet, I thought it most unlikely I would emulate the 'old man'! Instead I had Doug Walters caught by Asif Iqbal in the gully, a famous player and my first first-class wicket.

Fortunately, perhaps, the weather spared me having to bat, spared me competing with 151 not out. I say fortunately because cricketers do indeed sometimes pray for rain, perhaps as a break from the physical grind, perhaps because it removes the prospect of failure, releasing you from the public gaze.

My championship debut was against Derbyshire at Derby. I had gone up there to do 12th man duties, as young players often do, to benefit from a few days with the first team. A senior player not in the 1st XI at the time probably gains more from a game with the 2nd XI, while a junior can profitably soak up the atmosphere, and get the feel of goings-on with top players.

Half an hour before the start Graham Johnson collapsed in the nets with a cartilage problem. I was in. We won the match, chasing a total; I scored 14 and 35. This time I did not run out any of my side, but I did run out two of the opposition with direct hits and enjoyed every minute of the unexpected chance to play. In fact I enjoyed most of those early games with Kent, mainly because we were such a strong side that I was usually far from the centre of attraction. I sat around and listened.

Nor were there as many dressing-room comparisons with my father as I had expected. To make sure this remained the case I deliberately changed my game. My father was one of the best off-side players of all time, rightly remembered for his delicate caressing of the ball through cover, his touch play. So I played everything very aggressively on the leg-side. Unfortunately, during the two years I was becoming established on the first-class circuit I gradually lost all my off-side skills, relying on my good eyes to get me out of trouble. Cricketing cliché: it's all in the mind!

Secondly, so strong were Kent that I batted at seven, often arriving for a quick slog before a declaration or for a bonus point – a position or tactic to which M. C. Cowdrey was rarely subjected! But I liked number 7. There were advantages: I felt I could win games there, I felt there was a mental bonus too, an escape from exposure and responsibility. This, however, did hold me back as a batsman: no doubt I should have gone in earlier and 'played properly'.

The exposure problem increased after the innings I remember most. It was my first in the Benson and Hedges competition, the quarter-final against Sussex in Canterbury. For tactical reasons I

On my way to 114 v Sussex at Canterbury in the quarter final of the Benson and Hedges Cup in 1977. This was my first innings in this competition. My father scored 107* in his first innings – a unique record (*Patrick Eagar*)

M. C. Cowdrey (father of . . . !).
Question: 'Why don't you caress the ball through extra cover like your father?'
Answer: 'If I could, I would.' (*Patrick Eagar*)

was selected to open the batting instead of Graham Clinton. In the qualifying round Mike Buss had bowled his eleven overs for 17 runs, his gentle left-arm swingers keeping a nagging line and length. With my natural desire to play strokes, especially on the leg-side, the captain took a chance, giving me my biggest game so far. As an opener there was no hiding.

Fortunately we fielded first, helping a young player to shrug off some of the fears of batting. Sussex scored 264, a big total, but by tea we were 75-0 and I had already justified my selection. I slogged Buss for two sixes and edged the others for ones and twos, to be 35 not out at the interval.

We quickly lost Woolmer, Rowe and Asif Iqbal. 111–3 and our chances seemed gone. Then I watched Alan Ealham play the finest one-day innings I had ever seen, and we passed the Sussex total with three overs remaining. With 114 I was Man of the Match. The award should have gone to Alan, but as always he was the first to congratulate me.

The only blemish on the day concerned two comments in the bar afterwards. One was: 'You ought to get runs, with your background'; and the other: 'Your father got a hundred in his first Benson and Hedges innings, didn't he?'

I appeared on Nationwide in an interview with Frank Bough. As Son of Colin I was asked to join several chat shows. My telephone rang constantly. I had made one score yet was the centre of non-stop attention. Surrounded by Asif, Knott, Underwood, Shepherd, Woolmer, I was the person the press wanted to talk to, it was my 'story' they wanted.

Cliché: 'Cricket is a great leveller', and I was chopped down in the next one-day match at Maidstone. How?

I was lbw 0 to Mike Buss! I followed this with a run of low scores until I was left out from the final of the Benson and Hedges. Big disappointment. When you're on a bad run it's a killer, you can't see where the next single let alone the next boundary is coming from, yet not long ago you were Man of the Match, on Nationwide, on chat shows.

The pressure of public interest did wear me down. The most junior player in age and proven ability, I had been over-exposed. Slowly, very slowly, I adjusted. I scored my first championship hundred (against Glamorgan at Swansea), I kept going and in

1979 I was awarded my county cap. This was most important to me. In giving you your cap a county is saying: 'We think you are good enough. And expect you to remain good enough.' And this applies whether your name is C. Cowdrey or J. Smith.

Asif Iqbal in the Benson and Hedges Cup Final in 1977. I had a great respect for him as a captain and a player (*Patrick Eagar*)

[Jonathan]
I first met Chris when he was thirteen.

At Tonbridge, where I teach English, all boys are assigned to a tutor, which for us has nothing to do with the persistent pressure of academic life and everything to do with conversation and friendship. Each boy calls round to his tutor for a chat in the evening, a relaxing session once a week: coffee and cards, a laugh, a discussion, or a chance to unveil your latest hairstyle. In the summer you might go for a drive in the Kent countryside; in the winter you could watch TV round the fire or listen to your choice of records. Mixed in with all this is the really essential stuff: moaning, in-talk, scandal, outrage at punishment, keeping an eye on progress, or even asking (as F. S. Trueman puts it) 'What's going off out there?'. If a boy is happy, fine; if he's unhappy, the tutor is one of his best hopes.

Chris was a tutor boy of mine. As he says, at thirteen he was noticeably bigger than most of his age. He looked strong. He looked the sort who could run, throw, kick, hit, catch, a potential athlete if ever I saw one. He already prowled at the wicket or in the covers, with a ribcage in the Botham mould. But 'at tutor' we munched biscuits or cake and listened to Bob Dylan. Yes! Let's hear that one again. Neither I nor the other tutor boys could hit half volleys wide of mid-on, or crash them straight back over the bowler's head, let alone make brilliant diving stops, but we all liked *Mr Tambourine Man* and *Lay, Lady, Lay*. And even in his first year I noticed how good a mimic of masters he was, a comic gift which was to help him so much in dressing-rooms and on tours.

Above: Another hero! Alan Ealham is the best outfielder I have ever seen. Eyes on the ball, hands poised, front foot in the perfect position, and low to the ground (*Patrick Eagar*)

Below: Receiving my county cap from Alan Ealham in 1979

He is also quite right on a bigger issue: because he was called 'Cowdrey' he *was* treated differently. With him the other boys were either a little gushing or a little wary. No doubt I also treated him differently. Looking back I am conscious of being rather guarded, of steering the conversation away from cricket talk, yet aware there was perhaps a reflected glory in having a Cowdrey calling round to my place.

Over the next five years I had plenty of chances to see Chris's development as an all-round player, not to mention his exceptional skill in rugger and racquets. Especially in rugger I enjoyed watching his 'hands', his counter-attacking flair (he sometimes over-attacked, as he still does in cricket) and his sense of space. A natural in our own back yard. I was one of the many who gathered under the trees to watch his dynamic and powerful contribution to every aspect of cricket. Also I always sensed that communication of fun, that spirit of an entertainer which he has kept throughout his professional career. But what interested me as a teacher (and still does as a friend) is the balance of advantage and disadvantage in being the son of a famous father, especially if the son is also (and in the same field) very gifted.

I noticed, early in these pages, Chris's anxiety to hope he wasn't arrogant, recording how often at prep school he was slapped into detention for being 'bumptious'. Certainly the slightest whiff of arrogance from the very clever or the very talented or the 'son of' and some teachers unload their own special skiff of bricks.

Yet it's hard enough even for adults to adjust to being marked out as special and very few understand the intellectual or psychological demands that go with fame. It's difficult to absorb the pressure over the years. For every one who is keen to spoil you or chat you up because you're a Cowdrey ('Colin's eldest boy, you know') there's one who wants to cut you down. 'Cutting down the tall poppies' the Aussies call it (and the Aussies are extremely good at it). Then of course there are those who specialise both in chatting you up *and* cutting you down. So success brings attention and envy, adulation and snide carping. Sadly, especially at school, it can also mean that potentially the best friends somehow never even meet, they tend to keep away, not wanting to be seen as hangers-on.

To be educated at Wellesley and Tonbridge Chris was fortunate.

As a cricketer he was also lucky to have his father's expert early influence, then to be coached by many dedicated people and to practise his techniques on true wickets. He was given a great start, yet collected many uncalled-for remarks.

Whatever the influences, spoken or unspoken, as a cricketer he was remarkable. Things happened to him and he made things happen. Any game in which he was involved was less likely to be a draw. He is genuinely indifferent to statistics, with only the haziest notion of the details of major matches in which he has played, yet his record at both prep and public school is remarkable. And cricket (two more clichés coming) is about facts and figures, and his figures speak for themselves.

At Tonbridge Chris scored 2483 runs for the 1st XI, averaging 47·75, with five centuries. Two of these centuries were particularly memorable: 150 not out v Clifton – he prowled, he plundered – and best of all, 107 not out out of 157 v Wellington to win the match on a difficult wicket. The second was a schoolboy forerunner of his amazing innings for Kent in 1984 v Essex at Colchester. That innings against Essex was also on a difficult wicket (he loves bad wickets, loves the challenge, and admits he fails too often on good ones) and he made 125 not out out of 201.

His highest aggregate in a school season was 966 in 1975, averaging 80·5, captaining a side in which a fifteen-year-old called Richard Ellison opened the bowling. You can imagine how pleased everyone was when, nine years later, they played together for England.

David Walsh, the master in charge of cricket during Chris's last three years at Tonbridge, describes him concisely: 'A very strong player. His strength comes immediately to mind. He was a dominating influence, often in complete command, a man among schoolboys. He was astonishing in the field and as a captain. His assessment of the game was outstandingly mature, and I never doubted he would make the jump to first class. If you say "Give me one example", his innings at Wellington was the best schoolboy innings anyone on that ground had seen.'

This exceptional strength so evident at Tonbridge was to be seen in front of massive crowds a decade later. For example, in the 1984 Nat West Final at Lord's when he hooked Wayne Daniel into the Mound Stand for six, and in India later that year when he flat-batted Kapil Dev over extra cover far into the crowd.

My finest memory of him at Tonbridge does not concern a century or a quick fifty or a brace of wickets (he took over 70 with his seamers). No, it's a moment in the field, because anyone reading this will know Chris is one of the great fielders. (*Wisden* does not show who the great fielders are, but is there a better all-round fielder in England? Chris will say 'What about Randall, Parker, Gower ...?') Anyway, I can't remember the season, the match or the month and I was only watching the match for about fifteen minutes. I was sitting next to David Kemp, his house-master, on a bench, looking across towards the pavilion. My memory says it was a beautiful day.

The ball was struck firmly and well wide of Chris's left. He was at mid-off/extra. He seemed to anticipate the stroke, ran to his left, dived, scooping the ball up off the ground with his left hand, rolled over, transferring the ball to his right hand as he turned on the ground. Then, sitting up he threw out the batsman at the wicket keeper's end with a flat fast throw of about 35 yards from a sitting position. I remember standing up in amazement: the co-ordination, skill and above all flair. He believed he could do it. If you've seen him field you'll know his flair. He got to his feet, grinning, while the others whooped.

Over the ten years since, there have been many memorable feats: in the field, at short leg for England, at mid-wicket or slip, or in the covers for Kent. In one-day matches he is invaluable, making a contribution no score card can capture. And at the end of the memorable fourth Test in Madras 1985, Trevor Bailey said: 'Once again, Cowdrey was the pick of a marvellous fielding side.'

Also, Chris was quite simply the best schoolboy captain anyone had seen at Tonbridge. Masters and supporters from other schools said the same. Not only for the results he achieved but noticing the way he shaped and invigorated every contest. His success at school led to an unbeaten captaincy for Young England in the West Indies. (Interestingly, he mentions his anxieties about his selection for the tour but hurried on without saying he scored more runs than anyone, including Gower and Gatting.) This abil-ity as a captain has brought him to his greatest ambition so far: to lead Kent.

In the current jargon he is a 'communicator', whose love of the game and concern for the crowd's enjoyment shines out of him. As Christopher Martin-Jenkins wrote in the March 1985 *Cricketer*, 'he is thoroughly good for all those round him. A charming character, with *joie de vivre* tempered with common sense.'

Anyone who would wish to lead or to captain ought to remember that this is a vital gift.

David Walsh never doubted Chris would 'make the jump' to first-class. And in 1977 he did. Having been capped by Kent in 1979, he became joint vice-captain in 1982 and the following year had by far his best season with five hundreds, finishing as the second Englishman in the national averages.

Would he now make the jump to Test cricket? His 1983 season and a century v Surrey in Canterbury in August 1984 brought him special attention. But two 1984 performances in particular stand out, one of them on a small ground in Essex, one in front of a packed crowd at the headquarters of cricket. . . .

2

From Colchester to Calcutta?

I began Chapter One with a failure at a Kent coast prep school fixture. Why should I now suddenly hammer up the M2, join a jam at the Dartford tunnel and take the A12 to Colchester? Cricketers drive the length and breadth of the country week in week out all summer, so what's so special about Colchester, a small club ground with a bumpy outfield?

Well, some matches have a special significance whether played at Tormore or Tonbridge or Trent Bridge. A century can have a vital effect on your career or be simply one more hundred in a massive team total. A dropped catch may be a minor matter, soon put right by the next delivery, or it can cost you the championship. On this occasion in August 1984 Essex, the reigning champions of 1983, were once again top of the table and with Chris Tavaré on Test duty I was acting captain of Kent.

Not only were we without Tavaré, but much further depleted by a variety of problems. Richard Ellison was also playing for England, Alan Knott was unfit, Neil Taylor was dropped for disciplinary reasons and Terry Alderman, our Australian pace bowler, was doubtful with a hamstring injury. Not only Alderman but Jarvis too was struggling with a bad knee, and I had a suspected crack in a knuckle on my right hand, plus a cut on my forefinger which opened as soon as I hit a short ball, i.e. high on the bat. Jarring, a common problem for all batsmen against the rising ball, was going to be more of a discomfort than usual.

And all that was before I saw the surface of the pitch! Now, the preparation and nature of wickets is one of the most difficult and controversial aspects of the game, but if Essex had taken the grass off to comply with TCCB regulations – 'a wicket should start off brown and dry' – the ball would have turned square on the first day (and we had Deadly Derek). On this wicket, however, there was green grass and David Acfield, their off-spinner, was unlikely to be as big a threat on his own as Kent's Johnson and Underwood together. So they wanted a wicket to suit seamers, a track where grass dictates.

The wicket would clearly be the deciding factor and I am one of those who enjoy the challenge of a bad wicket. Anything can happen, the risks are greater, the excitement more intense – and results come. Cricket needs results.

Lastly our 12th man was G. R. Cowdrey. I had told him the night before to be prepared to play but not to bank on it.

On paper, then, and in everyone's mind Kent were the underdogs. Essex, with Gooch, McEwan and Fletcher were the top side in England, especially on a green wicket like this, with ridges and little bare patches. Their attack was strong: Lever, fortunately for us, was injured but they still had four international seamers, Foster, Pringle, Phillip and Gooch. (Including Gooch as an international seamer means I can now call myself one!)

What could we offer? A half-fit Jarvis, a half-fit Alderman, a half-fit Cowdrey, Graham Johnson, a young bowler Chris Penn … but there's always Derek Underwood, there's always Derek Underwood.

We won the toss. Without hesitation I asked Essex to bat, with the wicket at its greenest. Who on earth knew what would happen next?

Certainly not Essex. They were all out for 90 at lunch. The silence as we came off was an extra pleasure! The champions were all out for 90, partly because of the pitch, partly because Jarvis and Alderman produced 'on the spot' bowling, and partly because our catching was brilliant. (I remember being told at school not to over-use the word 'brilliant' but no other word will do.) As for the atmosphere around the ground, the stunned sound as the champions were hustled out by an under-strength Kent side, such moments are good, and with a side as strong as Essex, rare.

Were they expecting Kent to fold in the same way? Certainly, yet Ken McEwan had stroked the ball around, making the wicket look playable. So it *was* playable, and at lunch I told the team the wicket wasn't that bad, no, surely the point was: we had simply bowled superbly. *We* could get runs on it. (Cricketers are full of such theories.)

An hour later, at 3 p.m., Kent were 42–5 and the theory looked a little thin. Suddenly the crowd was humming, beginning to enjoy itself, and even more so – I remember the roar – when I sent Chris Penn back, he slipped and was run out, 47–6. When Waterton went we were 92–7, but if we could only squeeze a little ahead and give our bowlers just a bit to bowl at … Every run, every run mattered.

Tea 128–8. Eighteen wickets down by tea on the first day. Terry Alderman was playing a most courageous innings. He took some deliveries on the chest, then one severe crack on the elbow; he was hit by a bouncer, but kept going, scoring a run here and there.

Above: Terry Alderman. A fine example to those around him: full of guts and determination (*Kentish Gazette*)

Opposite: 125 not out v Essex at Colchester in 1984. A crucial innings in my career (*Adrian Murrell*)

Above: Receiving the Honeywell Award from René Berger and
Christopher Martin-Jenkins (*Adrian Murrell*)

Opposite: Eldine Baptiste. His selection for the West Indies tour of
England led to Alderman's signing. Two lovely guys to play with
(*David Munden*)

Only 18, but it was a feature of Alderman's cricket that when the stress was greatest he would deliver. On another occasion for Kent he survived nineteen overs at the Oval, including the fierce Sylvester Clarke on a lively wicket, and at Hastings he made 52 not out while Derek Underwood scored his maiden century, when all Kent's major batsmen had failed.

By the end of the Kent innings I was 125 not out. (Sorry about the 'Boys Own' story!) On a very dodgy wicket, against a fine bowling attack and with a painful hand I had kept them out. Every ball from Pringle hit the splice of my bat, forcing my bottom hand off the handle on impact. Any shot off the front foot I could play without pain. Of course to score a hundred on that wicket you needed luck. At first Neil Foster made me play and miss about twice an over, although it deviated so much and the bounce was so uneven I was probably nowhere near it. But I played better and better. Surprised to have reached even 50, I have never been so delighted with a championship hundred. Without any doubt it was my finest innings and won me the 1984 Honeywell Award for the highest strike rate of the season. (I did not know at the time but wouldn't have been surprised to hear that I would get 0 and 1 in the next match.)

In fact Kent were all out for 201, with that important lead of 111, which could win us the match. We took one Essex wicket before bad light stopped play, with Gooch still in to fight again.

On the second morning, it was clear it was going to be my game. Evidence? G. Gooch lbw C. Cowdrey.

Turning or leaping the ball was doing all sorts of interesting things. Once again the bowling was accurate. And the catching? Well, there's only one word for it. And just after lunch on the second day we had beaten the champions for the second time in the season. Underwood polished off their middle order when they looked as if they might wriggle away. At second slip I caught one of my best catches. Keith Fletcher was in and looked in quiet, unruffled control. As always he had played the spin masterfully.

Fletcher's was a vital wicket. Underwood applied the pressure in his relentless way until a delivery leapt off a length, took the splice and flew fast to my left. I caught it in two fingers diving backwards. I'm not sure what the word is to describe the catch but ... to be honest I was very pleased with it.

That victory was a vital morale boost at an important stage of the season. It also, finishing so early, gave us a day and a half off, vital rest, good news in the middle of a crowded few weeks, with the Nat West Final not far away.

[Jonathan]
Chris rang me in the West Country, where I was staying in a village with an even smaller cricket ground and an even bumpier outfield. I'd had an unsuccessful morning. After three hours of trying to write I had scored the novelist's equivalent of a long and undistinguished 0. Worse than that, like a batsman on a bad run, I was beginning to doubt I'd ever shape a decent sentence again. I stood up from my table and was about to take out my frustration on a couple of persistent wasps when the 'phone went. I hadn't yet seen the daily paper so had no idea about his 125 not out, nor Kent's strong position at the end of the first day.

'Jonathan? Chris here. Just ringing to say I've got you four tickets for the Final.'

I shouted the news out to the garden and heard the children scream and jump up and down. They rushed in from the garden, screamed again, and jumped up and down again. We're that sort of family. A full day out at Lord's, Kent v Middlesex, two fine sides, and four tickets together in the Mound Stand. Never mind the money, increase the mortgage. My mood was transformed. The wasps could live. My children? My children were no longer delaying my masterpiece but just naturally lively kids letting off steam and we'd all go for a walk round the lanes and play catch with a tennis ball.

'So, how's it going at Colchester?' I asked.

'All over.'

All over. Oh dear. He's acting captain and they've been thrashed by the champions by lunch on the second day. Still, there's always tomorrow, et cetera.

'Really?'

'Yes.'

Good though Chris is at not showing disappointment, he didn't seem at all low. Was there a grin behind the tone? I gambled he was holding something back.

'We *won*, you mean?'

'By ten wickets. No problem.'

There are few things sportsmen enjoy more than using the cool 'No problem' once they have done something minor like win the World Cup or climb Everest. It's a throw-away line, spoken quietly without emphasis, as if there's little doubt that result was always going to be the outcome of this particular encounter. Oh yes, we saw them off quite easily. Translated it means: 'We've just had one hell of a battle. And stuffed them out of sight.'

'But that's marvellous!'

'Yes, the lads are quite pleased.'

'The-lads-are-quite-pleased.' That's almost better than 'No problem'.

Next day the papers praised the exceptional skill and flair of his innings (next highest score was 18!) and the panache of his captaincy. Most of all, of course, on a personal level, the result added to the growing interest in his career, the sense that he had emerged from his father's shadow and that C. S. Cowdrey might himself play for England.

Botham had declared himself unavailable for the tour of India; Pringle seemed out of favour. Yes, it was a possibility. Chris was already known as a fine tourist, with a reputation for lifting morale, a one-day expert who could be an excellent influence on team spirit in all kinds of contest.

Nor was this Colchester innings a flash in the pan. Against Surrey at Canterbury he had batted against Sylvester Clark and David Thomas on a damp wicket. Kent were 17-3, 19-4, 42-5 before Chris scored 102 to turn the match into a Kent victory – and with the Duke of Kent watching!

The more I thought of it the more the Nat West Final 1984 began to look important, not only for Kent but for Chris's own future. Fail again (he got 0 v Somerset in the 1983 Final), fail in front of a packed Lord's on a big day, fail on TV in front of millions, fail in front of the selectors pencilling in their touring team for India, and Chris could easily slip away from centre stage. Canterbury and Colchester would be small entries in *Wisden*, nothing more.

Succeed, succeed in front of a packed Lord's, on TV in front of millions, and he could confirm a new phase of his cricket career.

Either way, the Smith family would be there to watch.

ESSEX v. KENT

Colchester, 22, 23 August 1984.
Kent won by 10 wickets

ESSEX

G. A. Gooch c Potter b Alderman	5	lbw b Cowdrey	8
C. Gladwin c Potter b Jarvis	6	c Penn b Alderman	1
P. J. Prichard c Hinks b Jarvis	22	lbw b Penn	37
K. S. McEwan b Jarvis	25	c Waterton b Alderman	44
*K. W. R. Fletcher c Johnson b Jarvis	0	c Cowdrey b Underwood	8
B. R. Hardie lbw b Cowdrey	8	b Alderman	0
D. R. Pringle lbw b Alderman	2	c Alderman b Underwood	1
N. Phillip c Waterton b Alderman	4	c and b Underwood	3
†D. E. East b Alderman	2	lbw b Alderman	3
N. A. Foster not out	1	b Alderman	0
D. L. Acfield b Cowdrey	4	not out	1
Lb 4, Nb 7	11	Lb 4, W 5, Nb 3	12
Total	90	Total	118

1–9, 2–15, 3–63, 4–63, 5–70, 6–79, 7–83, 8–83, 9–85
1–6, 2–32, 3–81, 4–106, 5–106, 6–107, 7–112, 8–117, 9–117

	O	M	R	W		O	M	R	W
Jarvis	11	2	45	4	Jarvis	7	0	41	0
Alderman	9	4	19	4	Alderman	12	2	27	5
Penn	4	1	9	0	Penn	3	0	8	1
Cowdrey	6·4	3	6	2	Cowdrey	5	0	10	1
					Underwood	10	3	20	3

KENT

L. Potter lbw b Foster	10	not out	5
M. R. Benson c Pringle b Phillip	4	not out	5
D. G. Aslett c Gooch b Foster	1		
S. G. Hinks c McEwan b Foster	0		
*C. S. Cowdrey not out	125		
G. W. Johnson b Phillip	15		
C. Penn run out	0		
†S. N. V. Waterton lbw b Gooch	16		
D. L. Underwood c Pringle b Gooch	1		
T. M. Alderman b Pringle	18		
K. B. S. Jarvis lbw b Acfield	0		
Lb 3, W 1, Nb 7	11		
Total	201	Total (0 wkt)	10

1–15, 2–15, 3–15, 4–17, 5–42, 6–47, 7–92, 8–104, 9–200

	O	M	R	W		O	M	R	W
Foster	17	2	51	3	Foster	1·4	0	10	0
Phillip	15	2	50	2	Acfield	1	1	0	0
Pringle	17	2	48	1					
Gooch	12	1	35	2					
Acfield	2	0	6	1					

3

Lord's Final: the greatest ever?

September 1st, 1984
I missed the Championship match (rested) before the 1983 Nat West Final. At Lord's I got 0. In 1984 I missed the Championship match (injury) before the Nat West Final.

Am I superstitious?

Once you win the semi (we won it in style) the tension starts to build. Players want to win the semi-final so much, yet if you lose you are – on one level – relieved that you're released from it all. In dressing-rooms I've sometimes sensed the feeling: 'At least we don't have the pressure. Now someone else can sweat it out.' But I always want to win, whatever the extra demands that brings. And I love big crowds. As for Daniel, Cowans, Edmonds, Emburey . . . I believed I could do well against them.

I didn't want to think too much about the Final until it was almost there, until the day dawned. It's a matter of keeping unnecessary expectation under control, keeping the mind right by not listening too much to 'Final chat'. I wanted to treat the occasion like any other match, which of course it isn't. Anyway, however hard you try to forget the big day you can't miss the announcements on the loudspeaker. 'Those who want tickets for the . . .' Friends ring you up, the club is in the news, the day-in day-out details are endless. Car park passes; who needs to be rested; who needs a physio; what about the dinner after the game; who's going to drive; where are the girls sitting. . . .

On the Friday night we travelled up in cars from Taunton (we lost to Somerset in the 1983 Final – bad omen?) and talked ourselves into a good frame of mind. But the moment I stepped through the hotel doors at 10 p.m. I could see it wasn't just another match.

Tom Graveney, Ray Illingworth ('This is a big day for you, Chris'), lots of old players, the press, TV crews, the feeling of being recognised, here-we-go, here-we-go.

'They've all come to see us play.'

Thousands and thousands will be there tomorrow, to see Kent win. I wandered round, looking for a quiet table, a place for a relaxing hour. But this wasn't a country pub. There was no escape. Not that I wanted one, because I like being with other players, I like their company before and after a game. I listened to the way they dealt with their nerves. 'I'm going to drink ten pints. Then I'll sleep.' (He drank one and a half pints and was in bed by 10.30.) 'I'm going to find a good night club.' (Also in bed by 10.30, *not* in the night club.) Others, the old hands more used to the atmosphere of finals, sat calmly chatting. Even at their table, though, there was a sense of jokey conversation, the jokes that cover anxiety. However experienced you are, when you walk down the steps to bat you're on your own. In the same way, however skilful or canny a bowler, when it's the last over and they want six to win, and the captain tosses you the ball, you are the only bowler. At that moment it doesn't feel much like a team game.

Will I sleep? Will I sleep well?

Yes, I slept. No, I didn't sleep well. I woke before my early morning call and was soon flicking through the daily papers at breakfast. They gave me considerable 'Son of' coverage, continuing the build-up of recent weeks. In *The Times*, under the heading 'Young Cowdrey makes a name for himself' I read:

'Comparisons can be odious, but they are inevitable. The most obvious difference between the Cowdreys is that whereas Colin persuaded the ball to the boundary, Christopher is always looking to propel it. The elegance of the former has given way to the adaptability of the latter in a different era and a changed game.'

The gist of most articles was that if I scored 50 or took 5 wickets today I could be a tourist. Most implied I was at last emerging from my father's shadow.

Well, am I? Yes, but I'm not that fit, my groin has been troublesome and I've spent the last three days at Taunton on the treatment table. Terry Alderman, none too fit himself, has taken to calling me Tables. So it's a pain-killing injection before we start, otherwise I won't be able to bowl my twelve overs.

I ate a good, proper English breakfast, as I normally do. (Do what you normally do before a big match.) It's a long morning session with a 10.30 start, and it is important to eat well and eat early. You need it to sustain your energy in the field and, whatever else happens, I do want to field well. I tell myself I can contribute there.

One good thing: we don't have to cart our kit over the road. It's there already in the dressing-room. We called in at the ground the night before and I looked out over the dark, empty arena.

At 8.45, after breakfast, we walked to Lord's, a ten-minute stroll along crowded pavements. By now there was a huge queue of supporters, some cheering us, some chanting, some giving us a bit of good-humoured 'wind-up'. I like all that. The police watched and smiled. Few fears of crowd violence at Lord's today.

And in through the Grace Gates.

On a big occasion I like to be early, unhurried. At Lord's, as you may know, the practice area over at the Nursery End is about five or six minutes walk away from the pavilion, and as we loosen up, and stretch, bowl and have a hit, there are still some big team questions. Is Terry Alderman fit? Is Alan Knott fit? (I am. Just about.) Instead of the twenty or so people normally watching our pre-match practice there are thousands coming through the Nursery entrance. More are gathered round the net I'm in than a total crowd at some championship matches. So it's an occasion already!

Then, warm and ready to play, we set off back over the magnificent ground towards the pavilion. I take my time and enjoy this, the packed electric feeling. Across the grass float the comments from the fans, the shouts of recognition and mockery. I can tell where the bulk of Kent supporters are, and I'm glad to know they're there.

10.00 a.m.

What will the captain do? Bat or field? I'm nervous but I'd be inhuman not to feel a bit of that. Back in the dressing-room it's twenty minutes of trying to find something to laugh over, searching for a photo in the paper, recalling a predictable comment by an old player, more or less anything to keep the pressure at bay. Are we going to bat?

A stream of people come into the dressing-room, committee men, friends, all wishing us well. Thanks. Thanks. Thanks. Are we fielding?

'We're batting.'

Terry Alderman plays. Alan Knott doesn't. Knotty comes in with Brian Luckhurst, having failed his fitness test. So it's Stuart Waterton to keep. We congratulate him. What is he feeling, pitched in at the last minute? If you wrote that story in a boys' magazine it would look far-fetched. For Stuart it means he can't sit down for the next two hours. (Well, not in the dressing-room anyway . . . .)

So we're batting. Pads on for the openers, a relief for the bowlers except it could be they'll be the ones under pressure at the end, in the extra tense final hour. At the death the spotlight will be on them. As a middle order batsman I feel some weight ease off me; I won't have to go in to try and win the game in the last twenty overs.

I look out from the balcony, wondering if all my friends are here by now.

[Jonathan]
Well, four of them are, for sure: the Smiths.

I woke at 5.55, before the traffic began. I woke because I heard some wild geese fly noisily over south London, a sound and sight I love. I pulled back the curtains, but they had passed before I could spot their formation over the crowded roof tops. My first bleary thought as I stood at the window was the terrified thought of the cricket fan:

'Don't tell me it's going to rain. Don't tell me that.'

No, it didn't look too bad, but nor was it a beautiful day, an ordinary, muted sky. Very English in fact.

Would those geese fly over Chris's hotel? Not a clue. I wasn't even sure which way was north.

We'd driven up to Balham the night before to stay with a friend, and to be sure of an early start we had already bought a big bottle of lemonade, Mars bars, cheese, coke, fruit, the lot. Loaded with sandwiches, binoculars, sun hats (well, you never know), ice bags and a few lagers ('Dad's got his grog, I see'), we set off for the tube. There were cricket fans all over the platform, laden much like us, and staring at the sports pages. Middlesex lot, by the look of them, and at every station we picked up more, all carriages bulging by St John's Wood.

The tube journey was long and hot, the last thing you want with a restless son. But grin and bear it and you're there, past the ticket touts and into the air, funnelling slowly down Wellington Road. The sky? The sky is OK, so-so, nothing to shout about, but it's not raining and that's the main thing. A mounted policeman goes by.

'No doubt about it,' the bloke behind me said, 'Knotty's something special.'

That's true, very true, and we didn't yet know the result of his fitness test. 'The buggers have closed the Tavern Bar, heard that?' We jostled and pushed our way round behind the high Mound Stand. 'Hang on a minute,' I said, and joined a long queue for a programme, thought it very slow moving and eventually realised it was winding its crocodile way into the Gents.

'When's it going to start, Dad?'

'10.30.'

'Is that soon?'

'Not long.'

'How long?'

'Quite soon.'

As we walked up the steps to K section and had our first view of the ground a posh voice on the public address system told us:

'For Kent, A. P. E. Knott is replaced by S. N. V. Waterton.'

K section is saddened. Somebody Special isn't playing, the Little Phenomenon isn't playing. We found our seats. Block K, Seats 0306, 7, 8 and 9. ('This portion of the ticket to be retained.')

I looked round at the settling thousands: people hailing each other, introducing friends, lowering carrier bags, lifting binoculars, people from every walk of life in every kind of dress: T-shirts, MCC ties, lightweight jackets, club ties, shirts undone, jeans, anoraks, beer guts and banter, Hoorah Henries and Watcher Mates, a loner with a big scorebook open on his knee and four different colour pens poised, a whole cross-section. I love it.

In the distance I can see two ex-pupils (not the two playing in the match) but as so often I can't remember their names. As always I can remember their handwriting. What that says about me annoys me. My daughter reads over the ad boards.

Texaco, Planters, Ladbrokes, Peugeot-Talbot, Gillette Blue, Gas is Wonderfuel.

So is the pavilion. It looks like a cardboard cut-out, clean and stark against the dull sky, something you could cut out with kitchen scissors from the back of a cereal packet. The brick is reddy-brown and the woodwork white as white. I search for the colour to describe the brick, fail, and turn to my wife. 'Terracotta.' Exactly, yes, that's it.

The Kent flag is flying and the hops are hanging over the balcony. I'm about to point out this little local detail to my son, explaining how the hops up there make the beer down here in my can when I see he's already tucking into our lunch. I tell him it isn't time for lunch yet, not by a long way, if he's hungry why didn't he eat a proper English breakfast (like Chris), when I remember that at his age I always did what he's now doing, and never got told off.

My wife focusses the binoculars on the Kent balcony. She makes out Alderman, Tavaré, Ellison, Underwood, Cowdrey ...

'There's Chris.'

All the family take it in turns to look and break off with the ripple of applause that welcomes the umpires, H. D. Bird and B. J. Meyer. Barrie Meyer I remember keeping wicket for Gloucestershire. After Wilson came Rochford, after Rochford came Meyer. Seeing Dickie Bird makes the crowd smile. Dickie has the seriousness of a dedicated professional and the potential of a naturally comic figure.

'Play!'

And the game is away. The first ball is always an event. After it we settle to the opening overs of Cowans and Daniel. Soon there's a cracking Taylor four. Crowd gasps. Tidy over. Benson looks very good off his legs. Daniel is quick. Definitely. Downton takes it high. A fine shot for nothing. Straight drive from Taylor. Nice solid start, nothing silly.

A good over from Cowans. He walks back towards our section of the crowd and waves pleasant acknowledgement of our applause. I like players who acknowledge your existence, who realise you're part of the day too. His white boots are as white as white can be. As a schoolmaster I approve. (I may not be able to remember names but I always check their boots.)

Almost an hour gone. Biscuit munching time.

'Apple anyone?'

'No thanks.'

'Penguin?'

'Yes, please.'

50-0. Benson sends his helmet back to the pavilion. Oh dear, I wish he hadn't done that. I wouldn't, never. Not only because I'd be scared to be on the same field as Daniel and Cowans without a helmet but because if ever I took off my sweater while batting and handed it to the square-leg umpire I was out next ball. Nemesis. One of those ever-alert on-duty Gods of Cricket said: 'Oh, that one down there thinks he's staying in for a while, does he? BAM!'

Still Benson hasn't got my hang-ups. But even forgetting the gods in the sky, won't that return of the helmet to the pavilion enrage those gods on earth, the quickies? Marshall, Imran Khan and Garth le Roux go berserk if you don't wear a helmet. It's an affront to their self-esteem, a serious slap in the face of their machismo. Send back your helmet when they're on and you're asking for trouble.

Ah, now this is interesting. There's a stir round the ground, a feeling of a controversial figure entering centre stage. Edmonds is coming on. Yes, yes, we knew it was Edmonds because he is telling Gatting where to move the fielders. Gatting is telling Edmonds where the fielders will stay. Edmonds is telling Gatting ... (Repeat sentences to taste). In body language it looks like:

Mark Benson (*top*) and Neil Taylor. Their opening partnership of 96 gave Kent a good start (*Kentish Gazette*)

Gatting: 'Look, I'm captain out here.'

Edmonds: 'Suit yourself, but don't blame me if there's a cock-up.'

Strangely, Edmonds, a great bowler, doesn't bowl well so is soon taken off. He seems to sulk. No, I'll rephrase that. He sulks. He seems to trip. No, he kicks the ground.

90–0. My daughter is filling in the scorecard each over, calling out this very encouraging total. On TV I expect they're calling it a 'platform' or 'launching pad'. Whichever way we're going well. I might have a drink in a minute.

'Who'll be the first to fifty, Dad, Taylor or Benson?'

'I don't know. Don't bank on anything.'

Chris must be relaxing by now. I swing the binoculars round. I wonder what he's doing?

[Chris]

Yes, at 90–0 I am relaxing. I feel better than I've felt all morning. There's a sense of quiet optimism up here on the balcony. With a bit of luck I won't have to go in before lunch. Yet one moment you can be pondering Mark Benson and Neil Taylor's technique and the next you're thrown in the deep end, almost before you can pull your gloves on. I've spent the last hour chatting, trying to keep balanced and even. I tell myself to play confidently when I go in, it's crucial I play confidently. Behind me I can hear Alan Knott telling Stuart Waterton to relax, have a sleep, you won't have to bat for a while. Richard Ellison, on my left, is taking it all in his big stride.

A roar from the middle. What?

Benson stumped Downton bowled Emburey 37.

'Nice stumping.' 96–1.

One of my team-mates is stumped by one of my oldest friends. Paul was at Sevenoaks, so we played against each other at school. Then we played together for Kent. Now we're against each other. In the winter, though I didn't yet know it, we'd be together for England. That's cricket, a crazy game. I start to pad up. Another roar. Not another wicket? Who's that? Taylor?

Taylor bowled Slack 49.

98–2.

That's exactly what we didn't want, two out in quick succession, but how often it happens. I'm next in. Bump, bump, faster beat, hands sweat a bit. I could be in before lunch, and I was beginning to think I might not have to bat at all. In before lunch? Out before lunch? Either way it'll be a long lunch. Instead of watching and pondering I could be on the receiving end. Or rather I hope the bowlers are!

[Jonathan]
My part of the Mound Stand is mostly stacked with Kent supporters. At the fall of the first wicket we didn't mind too much, a new face and all that, something to write on the scorecard, a new atmosphere. But 98–2 is a whole new ball game, it could be the beginning of a collapse. Will the headline in the evening paper read 'Kent squander early success'? We watch nervously as Tavaré and Aslett try to re-establish control. Aslett's stance is aggressive, as if he wants to get on with it, while Tavaré looks pensive and patient. (But I remember his brilliant 103 in the quarter-final at Taunton.)

'I want my lunch, Mum.'

'You've already had it. You'd better start on your tea.'

At lunch we stretch our legs behind the stand and meet Graham Cowdrey outside the Souvenir Shop. We discuss Chris but are both apprehensive, both hoping he'll seize his chance.

When Aslett is run out, 135–3, my children fight over the binoculars, to catch Chris as he walks out to the middle. He gets a big reception, revealing the depth and warmth of support he has in Kent. As he takes guard from Dickie Bird I wonder: does a professional *think* as he takes guard? Does he speak to himself in sentences or is it more a matter of snatches of emotion mingled with phrases of self-instruction, play straight, watch the ball, that sort of thing, the same panicky internal monologues we mere mortals do?

Overleaf: Mike Gatting and Phil Edmonds in a typical pose. The crowd at Lord's enjoyed their company (*David Munden*)

The game is in the balance, 135–3, with twenty overs to go, exactly the challenge Chris relishes. Kent must push ahead, and quickly. But think of the risks! As well as the game itself his own career is in the balance. The critics and commentators perched high up there in the press box. What will they say? Will he be pencilled in for India? Will he be the 'bits and pieces' player the selectors will take? If he plays well they might ink him in over the port this evening. I feel nervous for him.

Aslett's run out was on the last ball of Emburey's over, so Chris faces the first ball of Slack's next. Will he get off the mark or, as last year, collect a duck? He pushes it easily, a smooth controlled opening shot, square on the off-side for a long single. One run is better than none, a whole lot better, although some maniac from Middlesex immediately urges him back for the second. He settles for one.

Ah, good, Gatting and Edmonds are disagreeing again. It's hardly a private disagreement because if I can see it from K section, Mound Stand, the TV cameras can, which means that good old Gatt and our Henry are at it again. Arms are waving. If the sun was out no doubt we'd be seeing P. H. Edmonds's floppy hat hit the deck.

High above the scoreboard Father Time is not gesticulating, not even turning with his scythe. There's not even a breath of wind up there but the man in front refills his pipe and covers the whole of our row with a big cloud of embers. Embers! Through the smoke I can see Emburey spearing yorkers at Chris's leg stump. He digs them out. Good tense stuff. As always I am impressed by Emburey. When he finishes his tight spell, 12–1–27–1, we all applaud. Could that be a match-winning, controlling contribution? We'll see. Anything Emburey can do Underwood can do better.

Chris is on 12, the light standing out above his number, 5, just above the Peugeot-Talbot ad. If the small electric light shines that brightly on the board it means the sky is grey. If this was a Test match Dickie Bird would be revolving by now. And Wayne Daniel still has six express overs to bowl. I wouldn't want to face Daniel from forty yards in bright sunshine, let alone from nineteen yards in this murk.

Gatting calls up Daniel. This is the big moment, Daniel's second spell. Through my glasses, he looks very big, very strong, very dark and very fast. He is about to bowl at Chris Tavaré (27*). Inappropriately my daughter begins to read out more ads, Esso, Koda Colour film, Philishave, and suddenly Tav's gone, caught behind off Daniel, 28.

163–4. Enter Richard Ellison.

So it's the two Tonbridgians together. They played together for Tonbridge in 1975, now they're batting together at Lord's. Big, burly and unhurried, Ellison faces Daniel.

'Come on, Rich,' my son screams, with the fan's over-familiarity.

Ellison is off the mark with a 2 to third man. We cheer as if it was an imperious off-drive. The two batsmen chat at the end of the over, Ellison in a red helmet, Cowdrey in his blue. Chris hits a big four over extra off Edmonds; another four. And more.

Driving Phil Edmonds for four in the Nat West Final. Not exactly a classical stroke, but the right result (*Jan Traylen*)

Eleven off that over. Has he decided to take Edmonds apart? Edmonds looks at Gatting. Don't blame me, I didn't set the field.

'You can't do much better than that,' I say to my wife, 'eleven off the over.'

'You can,' my son says, 'Sobers hit 36 at Swansea.'

'Yeah-yeah-yeah, *we know*,' my daughter says.

'Now, *look*, you two, so far it's been a nice day.'

And it still is, of course. I'm enjoying every minute of it and now it's an even nicer one, a fierce pull from Chris through midwicket takes him to 37. He's racing away, playing the attacking game he loves, upping the tempo. Another four through mid-wicket, 200-4. Chris 46*. He's done his middle order bit well, but Kent need 250. A straight drive, that's his 50, must be, *no*, a diving stop by Barlow at mid-on.

'Come on, Chris, you can do it.'

Daniel bowls, and he does, the first 50 of the day. Are Messrs May, Bedser, Smith and Sharpe inking in the pencilled name? 209-4. Three overs to go.

'He'll be so pleased,' my wife says, and reflected glory washes over our family. I somehow refrain from standing up and saying to K section: 'I know these batsmen. Know them well.' And to reward my restraint we're on our feet. Chris hooks Daniel into the Mound Stand for six, just to the left of me. Magnificent stuff (but not as good as his run out at school) *and* the 50 partnership with Ellison. No sooner have we settled back on our hard seats than he's caught at extra. Cowdrey caught Radley bowled Daniel 58. 'Only Cowdrey', *Wisden* later wrote, 'had the imagination needed to break the bowlers' hold.'

232-6 at the end of sixty overs. Is it good enough?

[Chris]

I played pretty well for the 58 but I was annoyed to hit it straight at extra after that six. Instead of going for big shots I should have pushed ones and twos. Kent needed me there for the last two overs. I looked busy but I didn't hit the ball as sweetly or cleanly as I'd hoped. Still it's easy to criticise yourself. Whatever you do you could have done better, you could have done it differently.

Would I have settled for 58 when I walked out? Silly question.

[Jonathan]
Alderman opens the bowling. He's moving without his usual freedom. There's something withheld in his rhythm.

I look round the field: Waterton keeping (is he nervous?), Tavaré first slip, Ellison mid-off, Cowdrey mid-wicket.

Barlow tucks Alderman away but Aslett and Cowdrey combine

Hooking Wayne Daniel. A rare moment (*Jan Traylen*)

in a fine piece of fielding on the boundary, a reverse flick to Cowdrey who throws it flat over the stumps. With my binoculars I follow the throw and continue on to Derek Underwood down under the Warner Stand. Behind him there's a row of disabled people placed on the boundary, eight or ten of them, all part of the total scene. Four through the covers. 19–0.

37–0. After ten overs, too good for Kent comfort.

Big roar! Yes, Barlow caught Waterton bowled Jarvis, 25. 39–1. Well done, Stuart Waterton.

Ellison replaces Jarvis. Maiden from Ellison. Cowdrey replaces Alderman. Maiden from Cowdrey. Well bowled both!

Then a run out attempt. Close, very close! I imagine Ray Illingworth on TV is saying 'It's a bit tight, is that,' with his little laugh, as he watches the replay. You're right, Ray, very tight indeed.

Ellison bowls Slack, straight through him with a full-length ball, 60–2. Richard makes his way back to field in front of K section. We give him a returning hero reception. He grins, a shy grin, head down, like Princess Diana in the early days.

Chris has two shouts against Gatting for lbw, both turned down by Barrie Meyer. From where I am, 120 yards away at long-leg angle, I'd say they were close! 70–2 after 24. In Benaud-speak Elly's big away-swinger is working well, working too well, because the Middlesex lot keep missing the damn ball, instead of snicking it. (Statham, Hendrick, Ellison, me, it's always the same, why aren't batsmen good enough to touch our best deliveries?)

'*Yes*, Underwood is on!' my son shouts, having finished his tea. Deadly Derek Underwood, a living legend with a funny walk and middle-length run-up. First ball? What do you expect, on a length, where else, what other delivery would there be. Deadly doesn't need a loosener. And soon he starts to wear them down, as he always does, and it's no surprise when Butcher is bowled Underwood 15, 88–3. Now if he can get Gatting soon, I think Kent will win. Top Bowler to Top Batsman. Underwood gives nothing away, pinning down Radley and the confident, bustling Gatting.

> Good old Deadly
> He keeps on bowling
> He's just bowled Butcher
> He'll soon bowl Gatting

It's now 5.15 and the sun is out. Isn't that typical of the sun, to come out and help Middlesex, home team advantage, typical. Underwood chases hard after the ball, dives, stops it, picks it up and throws it in. Great applause, tinged with humour at Deadly's undignified dive. Would he, I wonder, have dived before all the Sunday League stuff caught on? 'The return of Arkle,' the wag shouts.

Underwood is controlling the scoring rate but Middlesex aren't losing wickets. We need wickets! Cowdrey throws the ball in, a head-high bullet which passes close to Gatting's helmet. Gatting and Cowdrey, friends and rivals, give each other a long glance.

'Watch it, Cow!'

'Just to let you know I'm here, Gatt!'

Closed Tavern or no closed Tavern the comments from the crowd are getting rougher, and more critical too when Tavaré, in a controversial move, takes off Underwood after nine of his twelve overs. Big Moment, this, is this wise? Underwood has three overs to go. Tav's keeping him back for the last part when the pressure's greatest. But they could have broken out of the stranglehold by then.

So it's Ellison again. K buzzes. Dickie Bird buzzes, it's getting quite dark.

Don't tell me he's going to offer them the light?

Gatting caught Tavaré bowled Jarvis. A fine catch. The crucial dismissal?

But Radley's still there. I haven't really mentioned Radley, who's played a vital, unremarkable, professional innings, but you wouldn't expect me to praise Radley at this stage, would you? On the contrary, the one-eyed K section wants his wicket badly. An aeroplane goes overhead and Radley is caught, caught Tavaré again, bowled Ellison 67.

Is that a match-winning innings or is that a match-winning aeroplane? Perhaps we need bombers. But Downton has, in his very composed way, played well, picking off the ones and twos, with time and a sense of controlled purpose (*and* he's ex-Kent!). Until Cowdrey catches him, off Jarvis, a friend catches a friend, funny game cricket, and suddenly Dickie Bird is hurrying round in circles, no, it's not the light, the umpires are off to the scoreboard, and shout up to the scorers. Don't tell me they've got the overs wrong! This is too much. And how can the scorers hear anything from thirty feet below when I can't hear my wife next to me?

218–6, three overs to go. While the scoreboard/umpire debate continues I wonder what Chris has been thinking and feeling the last hour or so.

Chris Tavaré applauds me for taking a simple catch to dismiss Paul Downton. Are Kent back in the game? (*Adrian Murrell*)

[Chris]

'Enjoy the occasion.' This is when the football manager's famous comment, said with a brave smile – 'Win or lose we are going to enjoy the occasion' – becomes so relevant. Standing out in a big open space at long-off in front of a full house with twenty overs remaining I must be calm. 105 runs needed, six wickets in hand, Radley still there, Underwood nearly finished – interesting odds. At 30-0 in bright sunshine we were struggling. With Middlesex 130-4 in gloomy light with Mike Gatting back in the pavilion I thought we would win. At 200-4, with the big Radley–Downton partnership, I thought we had lost. When I caught Downton off Jarvis we had a chance. Radley brilliantly held by Tavaré and we were favourites. A good shot for 4 by Emburey and they were favourites.

'Win or lose this is the time to enjoy the occasion.' Who would you rather be?

(a) Mike Gatting in the dressing-room, helplessly unable to watch the final over?

(b) Chris Tavaré marshalling the troops, discussing how Richard Ellison should approach his final over?

(c) Richard Ellison, who would be the hero of the moment if only he can restrict the batsmen to six runs or less off the last over?

(d) Edmonds and Emburey who had to find seven runs in terrible light, knowing that if one or other got out it was going to be terribly difficult for a new batsman to see the job through?

(e) The fielders, who now could hardly sight the ball in the general gloom, dreading dropping that 'simple' catch, but who could decide the match?

(f) Jonathan Smith in block K, who had supported Kent through the last eight and a half hours, and is as helpless to influence the situation as Mike Gatting?

(g) The umpires who, amid the bedlam and diminishing light, might have to make a crucial decision and then have it viewed countless times on TV?

As they conferred with the scorers as to who would win should the game be tied at 232-6, I conferred with my captain, Chris Tavaré, agreeing, disagreeing and finally agreeing. There were no rights and wrongs any more. Last orders had already been called.

'This is the time to enjoy the occasion.' Jimmy Hill might have had a competition on who would you rather be. My top three: (f) J. Smith, (a) Mike Gatting, (e) the fielders, but I'm not sure.

[Jonathan]
Right, my family agree on one thing: Middlesex need 15 more to win off three overs. As my children do the New Maths, which leads you to the wrong answer by the right route, this agreement is surprising.

Nerves are at full stretch on the pitch and in the crowd. Not a can top is cracking. The trouble is the two batsmen at the crease, Edmonds and Emburey, are experienced, cool heads.

'Come on, Jarvis!'

'Come on, Ellison!'

We slump at a dropped catch by Underwood, straight in, straight out, never mind, you can't criticise him, not after his fine spell and that chase and dive near the boundary fence.

Last over. Emotions yo-yo.

Ellison comes up from the deep fine leg boundary to begin his agony. No wonder this period is called The Death. Are his feet as heavy as lead, is he thinking clearly, what is Tavaré saying? Although Elly walks in a slow, measured way I can sense the tension in him. Absolute nail-biter this is, a field day for clichés.

Both sides have lost six wickets, both sides deserve to win. There's a delay while the field is set (Edmonds doesn't seem to object!) and here we go. The umpire turns round as if to say 'right let's play before it's completely dark out here'.

7 to win off six balls	1 legbye
6 to win off five balls	single
5 to win off four balls	two
3 to win off three balls	one
2 to win off two balls	one
1 to win off one ball	

The scores are now level.

Throughout all this the noise is a sustained hubbub of baying and advice, gasps and groans and no, yes, please-don't-get-run-out.

Last ball. If Middlesex score, they've won. If Kent stop them scoring they've won on faster scoring rate in the early overs. It's all on this ball.

Ellison runs in, Ellison to Emburey, a fine bowler to a fine bowler, and anything can happen. He bowls. Emburey hits it past square leg; that's the winning hit.

From all parts of the ground the crowd rushes on. We sag in our seats. It's all so unfair, winners and losers. As the players dash for the safety of the pavilion I'd like to see both sides walk slowly round the boundary to our acclaim, while Chariots of Fire plays loudly over the speakers.

'That's what it's all about,' someone behind me says sadly.

We collect our carrier bags and binocular cases and tread on crumpled beer cans. We walk through the debris and all the if onlys with spent emotion. If only, if only, if only. If he'd stopped this, if he hadn't snicked that, if that catch had stuck, if he hadn't slipped. But both sides can play the post mortem game. It's happened, it's all over, it's all written down in the scorebook, look in the papers tomorrow and you'll see.

The Smiths join the thousands who walk across the ground to see the presentations. I did consider dashing for the tube but we're not in a dashing mood, and it somehow seems a cheat to rush out on it now, you need the settling period, the moment after the hero's death and the final curtain while the emotions slowly find a steady level. And if we'd dashed I would have missed Clive Lloyd's funny remark in the gloom.

'I hope you can all see me down there!'

The fans laughed, peering up at the great West Indian on the balcony, as loyal subjects in the Mall look up at Royalty when they appear at the high window at Buckingham Palace.

Kent look stunned. They've been in the field so long, they're stunned and drained. Middlesex look happy. Chris jokes with Wayne Daniel. Good. Cliché: Kent didn't lose, cricket won. How did Chris feel?

'Very, very tired.'

We had left our friend's house in Balham at nine that morning. We walked back in, wearily, at nine-thirty that night – well in time for the highlights on TV! We had seen 120 overs bowled, 468 runs scored and the big final result resting on the last delivery. I'll never forget it, never. Had I seen the greatest one-day final of all?

NATWEST BANK TROPHY FINAL

Lord's, 1 September 1984
Middlesex won by 4 wickets

KENT

M. R. Benson st Downton b Emburey	37
N. R. Taylor b Slack	49
*C. J. Tavaré c Downton b Daniel	28
D. G. Aslett run out	11
C. S. Cowdrey c Radley b Daniel	58
R. M. Ellison not out	23
G. W. Johnson run out	0
†S. N. V. Waterton not out	4
D. L. Underwood did not bat	
T. M. Alderman did not bat	
K. B. S. Jarvis did not bat	
B 10, Lb 8, W 3, Nb 1	22
Total (60 overs) (6 wkts)	232

1–96, 2–98, 3–135, 4–163, 5–217, 6–217

	O	M	R	W
Cowans	9	2	24	0
Daniel	12	1	41	2
Hughes	10	0	52	0
Edmonds	5	0	33	0
Slack	12	2	33	1
Emburey	12	1	27	1

MIDDLESEX

G. D. Barlow c Waterton b Jarvis	25
W. N. Slack b Ellison	20
*M. W. Gatting c Tavaré b Jarvis	37
R. O. Butcher b Underwood	15
C. T. Radley c Tavaré b Ellison	67
†P. R. Downton c Cowdrey b Jarvis	40
J. E. Emburey not out	17
P. H. Edmonds not out	5
S. P. Hughes did not bat	
N. G. Cowans did not bat	
W. W. Daniel did not bat	
Lb 7, W 1, Nb 2	10
Total (60 overs) (6 wkts)	236

1–39, 2–60, 3–88, 4–124, 5–211, 6–217

	O	M	R	W
Alderman	12	0	53	0
Jarvis	12	1	47	3
Ellison	12	2	53	2
Cowdrey	12	1	48	0
Underwood	12	2	25	1

I sat on the bed that night drinking a coffee with my children crashed out asleep. I looked at the 15p scorecard faithfully filled in by my daughter. Blue biro, a child's hand and the corners curly and dog-eared. (It's in front of me on the table as I write this.) Chris said he was very, very tired. So were we, I can tell you.

[Chris]
After the formalities and the traditional sympathy I spent some time in the Middlesex dressing-room with Mike Gatting and Paul Downton. The losers are entertained by the winners. It isn't easy, that part, when you're still going through every feeling and trying hard to keep up a brave face. But it's important. One ball was the difference, one ball between winners and losers. What a disappointment, but what a game!

Mike Gatting turned to me.

'How do you like your curry, Cow?'

'Sorry?'

'Madras chicken? Prawn curry? Vegetable curry?'

'India? You reckon I will?'

4

India: out of the shadow?

To have any chance of success now, David Gower and his side will need to guard against the many excuses that will be theirs for the making: the umpiring, the boredom, the delays, the lost baggage, the lost causes, the unfamiliar food, the problems of communicating, the political opportunism, the soul-destroying pitches, the queasy tummies, the taxis that never turn up, the flights that never take off, the buses that are driven too fast, the invasions of privacy, the occasionally primitive accommodation. If the players are good enough they will overcome these things, if not they can still survive them with credit – and enjoyment. Take the rough with the smooth, that is the 'secret of India'.

John Woodcock, *The Times*, 30 October 1984

With those accurate words in front of us on the day we left London we had no reason to be surprised by anything that might happen on the tour. But even *The Times* cricket correspondent, even the Editor of *Wisden*, could not have predicted how rough the rough was going to be, and how long it seemed before the smooth arrived. First Mrs Gandhi was assassinated in her garden under a hail of sten gun bullets three hours after we arrived in Delhi. Confined to our hotel we looked out on the palls of smoke rising from the riots and reprisals in the city centre. With anti-Sikh violence unleashed how could we contemplate cricket?

We 'escaped' to Sri Lanka, and while a Hindu priest collected the ashes of Mrs Gandhi we practised in Colombo on a ground surrounded by tropical trees. Reassured and rested and with a monsoon to add to my experience, we returned to India and a revised itinerary. While we were away things seemed to have calmed down. Perhaps now it would seem a 'normal' cricket tour?

Far from it. Mr Percy Norris, the Deputy High Commissioner in Bombay, was gunned down 24 hours before the First Test.

Among the tour party, too, we had distressing news: Martyn Moxon's father died. Everywhere the pressure seemed to be on, everywhere we looked the signs seemed to say: 'This is no place to be. Go home. It's all a disaster. Get out before you get hurt.'

It is surely a tribute above all to Tony Brown, the manager, and David Gower, the captain, that the tour was so successful. If John Woodcock's analysis is correct then indeed as tourists we were 'good enough' because we overcame the effect of tragedies off the field and major problems in the games themselves. Over the taxing three-month period we gradually developed a pool of enthusiasm and determination which saw us through to a 2-1 victory in the Test series and a 4-1 domination in the One-day Internationals.

A number of interesting accounts have been published on the Indian tour. (Of those books I particularly enjoyed Vic Marks's effort.) So this is no place to write a detailed tour diary. Quite apart from anything else, I roomed with Victor for a fortnight, and it is clear from reading his pages that most of my good ideas have already appeared in print! So instead of describing the shock I felt on seeing the streets of Calcutta, or recounting an edited version of our Christmas party, I would like to offer six short sections:

  (i) A week in Bombay. My first Test.
 (ii) Delhi, the Second Test.
(iii) Jonathan Smith's views from England.
(iv) Madras, the perfect match.
 (v) The press.
(vi) India? An impression.

(i) A week in Bombay (rooming with: Bruce French). My first Test Match.

'Percy Norris has been shot!'

I lay on my bed, stunned. Another brutal killing, this time of someone who had entertained us, someone we had talked and laughed with only hours before. In a most friendly, informal 'do' Percy Norris had told Mike Gatting and me how much he would like to be a member of the MCC, how he wanted that more than anything. He mingled with all the guests and there was no hurry to leave this warm occasion. Well, he was now dead, killed on his way to work. Were we now the target? Would there be a lunatic at the nets or in the stands?

No one wanted to cut and run, but sixteen English cricketers in a coach on a busy Bombay street suddenly seemed a risk. We'd seen enough burnt-out buses after Mrs Gandhi's assassination, and all of us, in private, had our own fears.

We stayed in our rooms. Would it be safe to practise? With armed police patrolling the hotel how could anyone be sure what was brave and what was foolish? As it happened, with extreme concern, we went that afternoon to the Wankhede Stadium, and worked hard in the nets for a few hours. It helped to distract us. We were glad to be doing what we are best at, batting, bowling and fielding. And I was delighted to be told at 3 p.m. that I was in the 12 for the First Test.

I'm in the 12!

This surprised me. It surprised other players. It surprised the critics. And anyone could see I'd had a wretched month. 'Struggling' would be the word. Even before leaving home, while training to keep fit, I had been troubled by a groin injury. A few days before the flight I rang up David Gower to tell him my worries.

'But I'll be able to bat soon, I think,' I said.

'Good.'

'But it could be a few weeks before I can bowl.'

'Thank God for that,' he said.

With my record so far in India I couldn't see on what evidence the selectors would pick me. Indeed I'd become the subject of daily jokes, a regular fate for injured cricketers. This easily happens and can, after a while, get through to you, even if it's extremely good-natured. Graeme Fowler called me 'Prince Cowdrey of Canterbury' because what else was I doing except thanking the bowlers for bowling at me in the nets before retiring from the heat of the mid-day sun to nurse my slowly healing strain. I tried to laugh at this and other remarks, but the smile was wearing thin. My lack of fitness and form were irritating me. I like nothing more than being in the thick of the action, fielding, having a bowl, attacking the ball and after weeks of touring I'd been on the sidelines. Now, against all the likely signs, I was in the 12.

In the 12 but would the Test even take place? Was I going to be the subject of a silly quiz question asked in all the clubs of England.

'Who was selected in an England 12 in India but never played for his country?'

But, form or no form, I hoped to play. I wasn't going to fall for the escapist's approach, the desire to be 12th man and so be close to the action but not at risk. What's the point of running away from the big challenge, the thing you've always wanted?

In the eight o'clock bus the next morning I felt all the excitement of that first prep school match at Tormore, the sick feeling in the pit of the stomach. The Wankhede Stadium was empty at 8.30 with the gates still locked. In eerie silence we practised under Bernard Thomas's eye. Despite my lack of matches I felt good against our main bowlers.

Mrs Norris rang to wish us all luck. That impressed me so much, the courage and thoughtfulness of her message, given the horror she had been through.

'Right,' David Gower said, 'get switched on. Get your minds right. Paul Allott is 12th man. Bad luck, Paul. Congratulations to Cow and Robbo.'

Everyone shook my hand and soon, with black armbands on, we stood outside the pavilion for two minutes in memory of the murdered Mrs Gandhi and Mr Norris. The massive crowd was filling the stadium and stood with us.

46–0, England batting on an easy paced wicket. I was part of it all, in a Test match. Number six is well away from the front line, and I felt a pleasant distance from my debut innings. Always a foolish thought! 46–1, Fowler gone. 51–2 Robinson gone and their young leg-spinner Sivaramakrishnan the likely problem with his variety and control.

There's always a time when a batsman begins to be nervous. It has to come. You put on a thigh pad. When the thigh pad comes out of the bag you know you could be in within minutes. To keep calm I sat next to Norman Gifford, knowing his humour would take away some tension. Cricketers need chat and easy laughs and

Waiting to bat in my first Test match in Bombay. The black armbands are a mark of respect for Mrs Gandhi and Mr Norris (*Graham Morris*)

---

a friendly comfort to reduce the build-up. Reminding me of the hours I'd spent in the nets rather than in the middle he said:

'Now remember, Chris, when you hit the ball, don't go after it and pick it up.'

Roar. What's that?

Gatting out. Pads on.

I had the first pad on. I couldn't see the game from the dressing-room but from the volume of the next roar I knew it was a wicket. Lamb out first ball? ('It was', according to *The Times*, 'hardly a propitious time for Cowdrey to arrive for his first Test Match innings.')

I wasn't sure I would arrive at all, I was so rushed.

'Take your time, Chris. Take your time.'

I took a few deep breaths, put on my helmet, they wished me luck and I was down the steps and out into the bull-ring – or the concrete bowl. I passed David Gower – it was he who'd been dismissed. As I took guard I felt calm. Allan Lamb gave me a good luck nod from the other end and I asked the umpire how many balls of the over to go.

'Five.'

Five! End of calm. Five balls from Kapil Dev, King of Bombay, in my first innings. Wouldn't a quiet job in Croydon be much more sensible? Yes, but much less exciting and the statisticians wouldn't have been able to add Cowdrey to the list of Townsend, Tate, Hardstaff, Mann, Parks and Hutton, the line of fathers and sons who have played for England.

Kapil roared in off a long run. Full toss, leg stump. I hit it straight to mid-on. Damn! I should have scored off that. Still, at least I wasn't out first ball, but my feet didn't move well, a common problem for a cricketer when you're nervous. Being light on your feet is one of the most important aspects of batting, especially when you first go in. Sometimes you've been sitting down for a lengthy period, watching a big stand develop. Chris Smith does a quick skip with a rope before he bats, but then he has the opener's advantage of knowing when he is required, whereas I had rushed out feeling unprepared.

Even more of a problem with that first ball was its pace. Perhaps because I'd been so rarely in the middle it seemed extremely quick, similar, say, to facing Graham Dilley during Kent's pre-season training. However I survived the first over and pushed Kapil Dev through the covers for two in the next. I enjoyed those two runs, my first in Test cricket, but not the disappointment of seeing Allan Lamb out, spooning a catch to mid-on, Kapil's 250th Test wicket.

Richard Ellison is a close friend. We played together for Tonbridge School and are part of the same team at Kent. It may have been the West Coast of India but seeing him walk out, that helmet holding down the mass of curly hair, made me feel more at home.

Caught Kirmani bowled Yadav in my first Test innings for 13 (*Patrick Eagar*)

In Sivaramakrishnan's next over Richard was bowled by a perfect googly. 46–0 had become 94–6 and the critics would be saying it was all too predictable; last summer in England it was pace, now we were being undone by spin. 'Siva' already had four wickets with a style that reminded Norman Gifford of Mushtaq Mohammad.

Enter Paul Downton, ex-Kent, another close friend, and a determined character at the crease.

Who would have said, ten years ago when we first joined Kent, that Paul and I would bat together in a Test match. In between, in those chats that can help batsmen so much, I tried this thought on Paul.

'That's great,' he said, 'but I'm not sure about 94-6!'

Sadly, after an hour's batting, I edged an arm ball from the off-spinner Yadav to the keeper, 13. Only thirteen, and just when I was beginning to feel confident. How often every cricketer feels that. But thirteen isn't a total disaster, is it? Thirteen *Test* runs. In the coach on the way back to the hotel David Gower turned to me:

'Well, Cow - no one can take it away from you. It's Kent and England now.'

And while I rested the statisticians were still at work. Yes, the inevitable father and son first innings comparison:

M. C. Cowdrey c. Hole b. Johnston   40
Son of . . . . .   c. Kirmani b. Yadav 13

I didn't mind about the comparison but I agreed with David's press conference remark: 'We should be 250-3 not 190-8.'

29th November 1984

India passed our score of 195 for the loss of five wickets. They had taken a considerable advantage. I'd been fielding at short leg all day, with the helmet and shin pads on. Suddenly David Gower decided I was the man for a breakthrough. He threw me the ball:

'Get me a wicket, will you!'

Being at bat-pad all day, both ends, means you never run around. Your back tightens. My legs were stiff. It's an important place to field, of course, not only because of the danger of being so close to the bat but because you are always right in on the action, close to bowler, batter and keeper, 'keeping it going', always involved. Although I love fielding in the covers I was happy to take the close position: it meant less pressure on Mike Gatting, the obvious candidate for the job. Should the fielder at short leg suffer a bad blow it was better for the team that Gatting should not be the one at risk.

So, stiff and heavy-footed, I struggled in to bowl to Kapil Dev. Though weighed down a bit by my shin pads, which I didn't take the time to slip off, I did as the captain ordered. I got a wicket. My fourth ball nipped back off the wicket, one of those strange things that happen, although I don't know how or why. And I bowled the King of Bombay.

Kapil Dev (who can turn a Test match in half an hour) bowled Cowdrey. Not a bad first wicket. Disbelievers please see the photo opposite; for the statisticians I was proving a field day – did you know this made me only the 19th English bowler to take a wicket in his first over in a Test? No, nor did I!

At last I felt I was contributing something. From now on there might be fewer jokes at my expense, although the English faces in the middle of the pitch were amused at Kapil's downfall. Paul Downton grinned: 'I knew you'd get a wicket!' What is it about my bowling? Geoff Arnold always called me Boston, after the Strangler, because I have the knack of strangling a wicket with a bad ball, a ball which gives the batsman so many options he throttles himself.

But there was nothing wrong with the ball that bowled Kapil, however surprised my father might be. He was listening to this over on his car radio in London. When I came on to bowl he drove the wrong way up a one-way street. Fortunately the policeman who pulled him in shared the excitement of my wicket and M. C. Cowdrey was let off with a warning about his future conduct.

I rang him, heard of his brush with the law, and asked:

'How many Test wickets have you got?'

If Alan Knott hadn't misread a googly he bowled he would have had a catch behind. That was the claim. I can't see Knotty losing sleep over that one.

Kapil Dev. Bowled Cowdrey for 41. Who looks more surprised? (*Adrian Murrell*)

My Kent colleagues Knott and Underwood were much on my mind during the rest day; all their help, their advice on touring, especially the different mental approach required for India. And both said if I was picked for a Test I'd quickly develop a taste for it. With Kapil's wicket I was beginning to agree, but Sunday was bad. I was up all night being sick, and fielded at bat-pad all day. In the intervals I slept flat-out, totally exhausted. I shivered and coughed. Dust flew up into my face from the dry wicket and I spluttered away. The only taste I was developing was for Strepsils.

We bowled badly, they batted well and that night I slept for fourteen hours, 5.30 p.m. to 7.30 a.m. A night to forget, a day to forget, and with the ghost of Fletcher's tour stalking around, the worst still wasn't over.

In front of a huge, noisy Monday crowd we had to bat and bat for almost two days to draw. All morning I sat with Allan Lamb, obeying the cricketer's superstition of staying in one place if things are going well. While Gatting and Fowler fought it out and did their job, I wasn't allowed to move a muscle. Big roar. Not out. Big roar. Not out. Don't move, Cow! The crowd grew noisier, 35,000 people pleading with the umpire to give a decision.

In the last thirty overs of this crucial fourth day of thunder-flashes and frenzied appeals the decisions came. Gower was 'caught', so was Cowdrey. The umpire pointed the finger and I'll try not to. Let's leave it at that. I had shared in a stand of 47 with Mike Gatting and enjoyed the marvellous moment when he cut one through the covers for his first excellent and overdue Test 100. When he was in the 90s I tried to cool him down, told him to ignore the repeated bangs of thunderflashes, I wanted him to stop boiling too fast because you're more likely to survive if you keep an even mood. If he had been out going for the big hit I would have felt responsible for not seeing him through. In these small and often satisfying ways cricket is more of a team game than many realise.

For me the only consolation was the strokeplay of Mike Gatting's Test career best 136, and my Test career best of 14! We fought hard the next day but finished with the only thing we most wanted to avoid, defeat in the First Test. Typically, David Gower refused to excuse our performance on the pressure of the pre-match tragedies or on the umpiring. But there was already enough evidence to show how right John Woodcock was in the paragraph quoted at the beginning of this chapter. We had to pull together or fall apart.

Would we be 'good enough' to come back? Would the pitches from now on make results impossible? All round the place wise old birds were saying the same thing:

'You don't come back from being one down in the series, not on featherbed wickets, not in India.'

And in the press too. 'History', Matthew Engel of the *Guardian* wrote, 'is grimly repeating itself at Bombay.'

Oh well, we'll see.

(ii) Delhi, Second Test (rooming with: Vic Marks).

Travelling on the bus to Poona, yes a bumpy bus, with a row of Walkman heads switched on in front of me, I looked across at David Gower. I hoped he was enjoying a rare moment of being switched off from the constant attention and planning and anxiety a tour brings. Who would be captain of England's cricket team when things go wrong? Who blames Bryan Robson if our football side loses? It's obvious, isn't it: the manager must have picked the wrong side. In rugby league I can rarely work out who is the captain, while in rugby union the backs blame the pack and the pack blame the backs.

In cricket it's all put down to the captain. The middle order collapse is the captain's fault, he should have stiffened their determination. In that bad bowling spell after lunch why did the captain even consider putting that bowler on in the first place? A poor personal performance from the captain himself is the final nail. If you're an England captain no mistake will go unnoticed. Succeed and there is great glory, your photo will move from the back pages of the press to the front, but you must have a team capable of success.

Were we capable of success?

On the bus ride to Poona we all had our worries. David had five uncomfortable hours to ponder our chances on the rest of the tour. For myself I hoped I'd make a big contribution in the One-day International, but I was promptly left out. This surprised me as much as my inclusion in the First Test because my tour place was based presumably not only on Peter May's 'hunch' but on my reputation in one-day cricket. I was called the 'bits and pieces' player, which some players find an insulting definition. It doesn't bother me; in fact I rather like it.

Whatever my thoughts – the slumping feeling that I'd miss the intense involvement – the selection was justified. We won the first One-day International among a shower of fruit and lemonade bottles from the crowd. This victory, this compensation, brought a vital change of mood before we went back to Bombay for the North Zone fixture. Here I took my chance with 70, but this time the Wankhede Stadium was almost empty with none of that claustrophobic feel of the First Test. Still, the press suggested Martyn Moxon and I were competing for that last place. Maybe that was true. Martyn, playing for the first time on tour, scored 42 and the match ended in a flat draw.

So we headed back for Delhi, another five hours on another bumpy bus back to Delhi, where five weeks earlier our tour had almost ended. And we arrived two hours late! John Woodcock's prediction on flights and baggage proved exactly right, but we were determined to seize the initiative, a determination strengthened by a feeling we'd been unlucky with decisions.

12th December 1984. Second Test.   Played at Ferozshah Kotla
'There are big cracks all over the wicket and the cracks feel loose.' 'It looks like motorway concrete.' 'It's uneven. It'll get worse.' Everyone stared and prodded at the pitch. John Thicknesse, of the *Evening Standard,* was as usual running the book and preparing his odds. He was predicting no play at all on the fifth day: this game was vital to his pocket!

I did my stretching exercises, wondering if my place would go to Vic Marks, my room-mate and rival author. I kept my place and Vic kept his disappointment well hidden.

The odds quoted in the press box were 4 to 1 against an England victory. Well though we played throughout the game, an England victory did not look likely at lunch on the fifth day. True, by then everyone had done something: Tim Robinson's single-minded 160 in eight and a half hours; Richard Ellison dismissed Gavaskar for one with his perfect outswinger; Phil Edmonds drifted the ball with great skill; Paul Downton notched up an important 74;

Norman Cowans's hostile burst at the beginning of their second innings shook up the top Indian order.

What had I done?

Well, I had run 40 yards back from leg gully trying to reach Vengsarkar's mishook off Cowans. I dived full length, got all my fingers to the ball but not much hand. What would have been my finest catch was not to be.

My batting? I kept my pads on for the whole lunch break, explaining to Paul Downton that I was trying to get the feel of a long innings. And this wasn't altogether a joke: I was determined. I fought hard against their accurate spinners for half an hour then decided to enjoy my naturally aggressive game. (Vic Marks said I suddenly played as if I was wearing my Kent sweater!) I hit Yadav through the covers for four and over mid-wicket for six.

Driving Yadav through extra cover in Delhi (*Patrick Eagar*)

While Tim Robinson picked up singles and hit the half-volley, I felt free to bat the way I wanted to. It was risky but fun. I hit Sivaramakrishnan over long-on for six. It was a googly and I saw it.

Opposite: Tim Robinson. His magnificent 160 in the 2nd Test in Delhi set up our victory (*Graham Morris*)

Below: Six over wide mid-on. Well . . . mid-wicket! (*Patrick Eagar*)

Above: As you can see from the other expressions I am rather overdoing the congratulations. Graeme Fowler often applauded me for relatively simple stops at short-leg, so I am returning the compliment after he had taken a very easy catch! (*Adrian Murrell*)

Opposite: Slogging Siva over mid-on for 6 (*Graham Morris*)

There was little doubt we were getting on top. Siva ran up with less enthusiasm, but my pleasure wasn't to last. A leg spinner landed full on my boot, looped to gully and I was given out. Caught Gavaskar! The disappointment I felt, dismissed in that fashion on 38, was desperate. All my attempts to establish myself, to justify the selectors' hunch in picking me for the tour, my hopes of making a major and vital contribution to the team effort, seemed in ruins. Among other things, and other people, I blamed my big feet. That night, though, I told myself it would be bad to believe I was fated, that's a hopeless frame of mind for a cricketer.

SECOND TEST MATCH

Delhi, 12, 13, 15, 16, 17 December 1984   England won by 8 wickets

INDIA

*S. M. Gavaskar c Downton b Ellison	1	b Pocock	65
A. D. Gaekwad b Pocock	28	c Downton b Edmonds	0
D. B. Vengsarkar st Downton b Edmonds	24	b Cowans	1
M. Amarnath c Gower b Pocock	42	b Edmonds	64
S. M. Patil c Pocock b Edmonds	30	c Lamb b Edmonds	41
R. J. Shastri c Fowler b Pocock	2	not out	25
Kapil Dev c Downton b Ellison	60	c Lamb b Pocock	7
†S. M. H. Kirmani c Gatting b Ellison	27	b Pocock	6
M. Prabhakar c Downton b Ellison	25	c Downton b Cowans	5
N. S. Yadav not out	28	c Lamb b Edmonds	1
L. Sivaramakrishnan run out	25	c and b Pocock	0
B 1, Lb 12, Nb 2	15	B 6, Lb 10, W 1, Nb 3	20
Total	307	Total	235

1–3, 2–56, 3–68, 4–129, 5–131, 6–140, 7–208, 8–235, 9–258

1–12, 2–15, 3–136, 4–172, 5–207, 6–214, 7–216, 8–225, 9–234

	O	M	R	W		O	M	R	W
Cowans	20	5	70	0	Cowans	13	2	43	2
Ellison	26	6	66	4	Ellison	7	1	20	0
Edmonds	44·2	16	83	2	Edmonds	44	24	60	4
Pocock	33	8	70	3	Pocock	38·4	9	93	4
Gatting	2	0	5	0	Gatting	1	0	3	0

ENGLAND

G. Fowler c Gaekwad b Prabhakar	5	c Vengsarkar b Sivaramakrishnan	29
R. T. Robinson c Gavaskar b Kapil Dev	160	run out	18
M. W. Gatting b Yadav	26	not out	30
A. J. Lamb c Vengsarkar b Yadav	52	not out	37
*D. I. Gower lbw b Sivaramakrishnan	5		
C. S. Cowdrey c Gavaskar b Sivaramakrishnan	38		
†P. R. Downton c Kapil Dev b Sivaramakrishnan	74		
P. H. Edmonds c Shastri b Sivaramakrishnan	26		
R. M. Ellison b Sivaramakrishnan	10		
P. I. Pocock b Sivaramakrishnan	0		
N. G. Cowans not out	0		
B 6, Lb 13, Nb 3	22	B 4, Lb 7, W 2	13
Total	418	Total (2 wkts)	127

1–15, 2–60, 3–170, 4–181, 5–237, 6–343, 7–398, 8–411, 9–416

1–41, 2–68

	O	M	R	W		O	M	R	W
Kapil Dev	32	5	87	1	Kapil Dev	6	0	20	0
Prabhakar	21	3	68	1	Prabhakar	3	0	18	0
Sivaramakrishnan	49·1	17	99	6	Sivaramakrishnan	8	0	41	1
Yadav	36	6	95	2	Yadav	2	0	7	0
Shastri	29	4	44	0	Shastri	4	0	20	0
Amarnath	2	0	6	0	Gavaskar	0·4	0	10	0

Still, at lunch on the fifth day, with India at 204-4, we gamblers felt England had just the hint of a chance. Although the wicket had held together, the new ball was available in the afternoon; I felt we should take it. David Gower disagreed. He decided to give them no possible respite, to plug away with Edmonds and Pocock. He was rewarded, wickets coming at just the right time. India slumped: 207-5, 214-6, 216-7, 225-8, 234-9, 235 all out.

First Patil, then Kapil Dev played astonishingly reckless shots. But it's easy to say that, and I've been part of many batting collapses. Phil Edmonds changed his pace and flight with subtle effect, returning 44-24-60-4 and Pat Pocock took the wickets of Gavaskar, Kapil, Kirmani and Siva. In ninety minutes India lost six wickets and England wanted only 125 to win.

Again I had an annoying moment with a good catch at forward short-leg turned down, but it was all forgotten in the great excitement of levelling the series. Instead of England in the firing line it was now India in disarray. Kapil, the hero of Bombay, was dropped for the manner of his dismissal (giving Pocock the charge, caught deep mid-off) and happily the English critics now turned on the indiscipline of the Indian team.

'One now associates the kind of ghastly batting performance they produced yesterday with England players.' – Matthew Engel, the *Guardian*

'Abject surrender' – Richard Streeton, *The Times*

Siva had taken nineteen wickets already in the Tests but there was a genuine feeling now in the tour party that we were getting to grips with him, that he was vulnerable to attack and that he could be made to pay in the following matches.

In the final overs I sat back and watched Gatting and Lamb slam a succession of boundaries. We had levelled the series, we had ended the drought, we drank some John Smith's bitter, we had not allowed the ghost of the past to haunt us. Above all we felt pleased for David Gower who had gained his first win in eleven Tests as England's captain. Future journeys would not be as grim as the bus to Poona.

We flew to play East Zone at Gauhati in Assam, a pleasant break from Test arenas and a chance to rest and watch the Gavaskar–Kapil ('No Kapil – No Test') row. We won at Gauhati too. Win one, win two. Win two, win three.

'Here we go, here we go, here we go . . .'

Perhaps we could put away the Walkmans and have a sing-song?

(iii) India from England: Jonathan Smith's view

They left on the day the clocks went back but I followed the England cricketers from city to city all over India. Not on my bicycle like some, but in my mind's eye. In recent years I have read a fair few stories set there, novels by Paul Scott, Anita Desai, Ruth Prawer Jhabvala and of course E. M. Forster (Old Tonbridgian!) but I've never been to India myself. If you gave me an outline map and told me to fill in all the main cities I wouldn't have a clue. (That map exercise was in fact a punishment in the first school I taught at.)

With a sense of deep ignorance and only the haziest notion of the sub-continent's geography, I traced and zig-zagged the team's busy itinerary, first along their original tour plan and, after Mrs Gandhi's death, the hastily revised version. I traced it out on the big pages of the *Times World Atlas*. I also borrowed a guide from the town library. In the long winter evenings at home we would sometimes lean over the heavy Atlas and find Gauhati or Jaipur or Calcutta and read out whatever the guide said. While this serious research continued my son stood in front of the TV with his bat muttering 'And it's Kapil Dev to Chris Cowdrey and he smashes it for six.' (He did precisely that, too – over extra cover, in the fourth One-day International.) One sad, horrified night, after watching the news on TV I found Bhopal, a place never considered on the tour. Bhopal. How relieved we were that our players were so far from those unspeakable scenes of gas, blindness and death.

It occurred to me later, talking to Chris on his return, that by reading we probably knew more about the area he was in than he did himself: cricketers on tour tend to see airports, they attend functions, sleep in hotels, play cards, cluster in dressing-rooms, complain about umpires, bend over snooker tables, push baggage trolleys and smell Calcutta from the inside of a bus. Whereas by playing Chris's tapes, listening to the BBC match commentaries, the occasional 'phone call and visiting the library, I felt somehow very in touch. Involved even.

On early December or January mornings, with black ice outside and no doubt a two-mile tailback at the Dartford tunnel, I would very quietly tune into Radio 3 Medium Wave, hoping I wouldn't wake my wife. In class, if an exciting session was in progress I would sometimes put aside Sassoon's *Memoirs of an Infantry Officer*, leave the clay of the First World War trenches and slip over to Madras, especially if Chris was bowling. He reeled off fourteen on the trot there, overs 'prodigious in their endeavour' (John Woodcock). After all, Tonbridge is a cricket-mad school, let's face it, and with Ellison and Cowdrey on the tour we felt forgivable pride. There were no complaints from my pupils, nor (as far as I know) from their parents, about my unprofessional conduct.

When Chris was out we groaned. In Delhi he was cut down in full flow. After hitting those sixes he was caught Gavaskar bowled Sivarama, 38. Caught off his boot, the commentator said: 'What's the point!' I complained, feeling angry and upset from 7,000 miles away. Was he kicking the ground as he walked out or did he stumble? What was next on the agenda? Caught off your ear?

When he bowled Azharuddin or took Kapil's wicket we cheered. All right, on paper his achievements in India do not look impressive, but we all held our breath each time he played.

As the First Test came up Chris was, as he has written, unlikely to be picked. He was picked. And from that moment his number six spot was always under discussion and threat. Would they play an extra batsman – Moxon or Marks? 'Cowdrey surprise selection!' Would he be dropped after the First Test? No. One – two – three – four – five. Bombay – Delhi – Calcutta – Madras – Kanpur – he hung in there. Assuming this selection pattern wasn't all a public school plot, an interesting picture emerges. His attacking potential with the bat was obviously a bonus, his brilliance in the field a boon, particularly in India where he spent endless alert hours fielding not in his natural position but sweltering under the helmet at bat-pad, motivating bowlers, lurking ready to snaffle the chances off Pocock or Edmonds. When he recovered from his groin injury he helped out with the bowling too, especially in Madras with his grittily determined spell. It was very gratifying later to read in Vic Marks's book: 'After four hours we sensed a golden opportunity to snatch a Test Match victory, thanks to the bowling of Foster and Cowdrey.'

Opposite: Keeping the chat going from short-leg (*Graham Morris*)

Below: 3rd Test match. Calcutta. Catching Amarnath off Phil Edmonds. Not a very difficult chance, but you have to wait a long time at short-leg so it's always nice to hold on to it (*Graham Morris*)

But these factors are not, I believe, the most convincing justification for Chris's inclusion. Putting aside for one moment his gifts, the main reason anyone would want Chris Cowdrey in a side is his flair for the game, his feeling for the spirit of it all, his effect on his team's morale.

Such a remark might well make many cricketers smile. 'Team spirit? Team awareness? Don't make me laugh! It's all about individuals.' Many see the game as 'work', as a contest in which the side with the greater fire power, particularly in fast bowling, wins. Full stop.

Well, maybe, but I'm not so sure. If a player has the right spirit and natural instinct for cricket it can affect others for the good. How often a moaner can drag down others in the dressing-room, carping and destroying, chipping away. Whereas a man who can draw out the best feelings and combat depression, who encourages others to fulfil their potential – his balance and positive involvement can lift us all.

Listening in those early hours in bed I noticed how often Jack Bannister or Peter Baxter or Trevor Bailey referred to 'Cowdrey, an excellent tourist'. His personality off the field, his sense of fun, was frequently praised; and the television highlights showed him in the thick of things, encouraging everyone else.

His spirits did indeed keep him in the Test side throughout the series. And England's team spirit in India 1984/5 has been widely recognised as one of the party's greatest strengths, possibly the prime reason why, against all the odds, and one down, it was finally victorious.

And what a thrill that second victory, in Madras, gave us. Even in the worst of winters there's a spring in your step when the England cricketers are doing well. Rain, snow, black ice simply don't matter when there are Tests like Madras on the radio. 'Doing it for those back home' really does mean something, and is based on solid, deep-seated evidence. Jeremy Cowdrey on The Stock Exchange was giving his clients the score as well as advice. Every car radio was on, going up and down one-way streets. Every school had a radio tuned in, briefly of course, in the middle of lessons.

Runs, wickets, catches, statistics, they're all very important. But to insist only on that evidence, to say in the current jargon 'That's what it's all about', is a reduction of the human value and subtlety of the game.

(iv) Madras, the perfect Test

Madras, the decisive Test, the perfect Test.

Why? First of all the contrast. It followed the slow tedious draw of the Third Test at Eden Gardens, Calcutta. It contained four astonishing innings (by Fowler, Gatting, Amarnath and Azharuddin), an opening stand of 178 for England, an eleven-wicket haul for Neil Foster and, most important of all, we won by nine wickets.

Was it perfect or decisive for me too? No, but I caught three catches – Shastri, Srikkanth and a good one, knocking up a firm hook by Siva. I bowled 24 overs and took the wickets of the dashing Azharuddin and of Kapil Dev. And when I batted I was 3 not out. Not perfect, but I've done worse.

To be honest, we were very glad to leave Calcutta, and not just the dust and the smog, the smell of the rubbish tips and the grim squalor of the side streets. Christmas is never an easy time on tour, with homesickness at its most obvious. You don't wake up looking for a stocking at the end of your bed and people can be quite touchy under the forced merriment. I woke up with sketches and songs running round in my head, but at least the Social Committee (Fowler, Marks and Cowdrey) thought the entertainment they provided for the tour party was top-quality stuff. For the publishable details see Vic Marks's book; for the better bits speak to me in a sponsor's tent.

Was anything else good about Calcutta? There was the big Richard Ellison (Bill Webernuik) v Chris Cowdrey (Kirk Stevens) clash at snooker. There was Phil Edmonds reading a newspaper in the outfield as a protest against Gavaskar's decision to bat on and on, so killing any chance of a game. There was Allan Lamb's 67 and the sight of him in a policeman's helmet at third man. And the sound of Mike Gatting after I'd locked him out of our room and fallen into a very deep sleep: it's just that I had had enough in the bar, and more than enough of Gatting playing Tina Turner's 'Private Dancer'. And of course Richard Ellison's fifty-three overs, an heroic effort with no luck at all.

Above: Dismissing Azharuddin in Madras. This gave me great
satisfaction as we had found him hard to get out. It is extraordinary
how the stumps have gone sideways. Sheer pace! (*Graham Morris*)

Opposite: Walking back to bowl in the 4th Test at Madras. This is a
favourite picture: dirty trousers, sweating profusely. It shows I have
been involved in the battle (*Adrian Murrell*)

But on balance the Third Test was a predictably dull, grim
game and one which convinced Sunil Gavaskar he never wanted
to play in Calcutta again. We weren't sure we wanted to either.
   Eight days later we were in Madras, much better all round, and
never a dull moment. Madras, Sivaramakrishnan's home town,
produced a colourless wicket that bounced a bit early on. And the
ball swung. Neil Foster came into the side instead of Richard

Ellison and it was Neil who did the damage. Gavaskar, Srikkanth and Vengsarkar were all gone at 45. 45-3 and the Indian counter-attacking approach to the new ball bowling had failed. Fossie's high action, right arm right over the top, found the vital steep bounce and everything was going on at the double, runs, wickets, all action. My kind of game in fact, and there was more to come.

Amarnath and 'Azza' now played a series of uninhibited shots against our quick bowlers and even Phil Edmonds, the central controlling strength of our attack throughout the long tour, was hit for four successive boundaries. We were chasing the ball all over the lightning fast brown outfield on a scorching day. These two, hooking and cutting, put on 110 runs in no time. Azza, as so often in the series, looked magical.

During this fine stand, David Gower, perhaps feeling he had no other option left, turned to me.

'You mean I'm a first change seamer? You mean I'm the third seamer in the England side?'

'No, I mean there's no one else, mate.'

Oh well.

This time, though, I didn't have a brief bowl, a brief moment of glory or humiliation and then off. This time I was really given a spell. In the game before the Fourth Test I had bowled well in Hyderabad against South Zone. In thirty-three overs I took four wickets. The 'Prince' nickname had died a very slow death on the tour, so I worked hard through the sticky Madras mid-day and afternoon heat. In the first innings I bowled nineteen overs and dismissed Azharuddin and Kapil Dev. 'To everyone's surprise,' Marks wrote, 'Cowdrey bowled Azharuddin.' What a way for one member of the Social Committee to write about another! In fact, Victor, I dismissed him three times on the tour, although whether that makes each dismissal more or less amazing I'm not quite sure.

Whatever, India were all out for 272. If we could now 'bat for two days', the famous advice of all captains, the Test could be ours. A scoreboard of England 419-1 was enough to show us we were likely to win the match, a demo job which proved that Siva was no longer dominant, and by the time Gower declared with a massive score of 652-7, two English batsmen had scored double centuries in the same innings, a feat never before achieved. When the ball was there to be hit they hit it; when an hour's steely concentration was needed Fowler and Gatting found it. We had come a long way from Bombay, and I'll never lock Gatting out again.

There is a special pleasure for all games players in being asked to do something you don't normally do. At Madras I was given the ball *as a bowler*, not just as someone who would help out or possibly break a stand. I enjoyed Madras so much, not only because of the talent of my team-mates but because I was intensely involved on the pitch. Also, of course, I was given a long spell, and because the quick bowlers (Foster and Cowans) were on so much, I wasn't fielding all day at bat-pad, my usual tour position for the spinners. I was free, running round at square leg and diving for the ball. I watched Graeme Fowler chase a ball, turn a four into a three, and I looked for every opportunity to do the same.

Catching Srikkanth off Neil Foster's bowling. One of Fossie's 11 wickets in the match (*Graham Morris*)

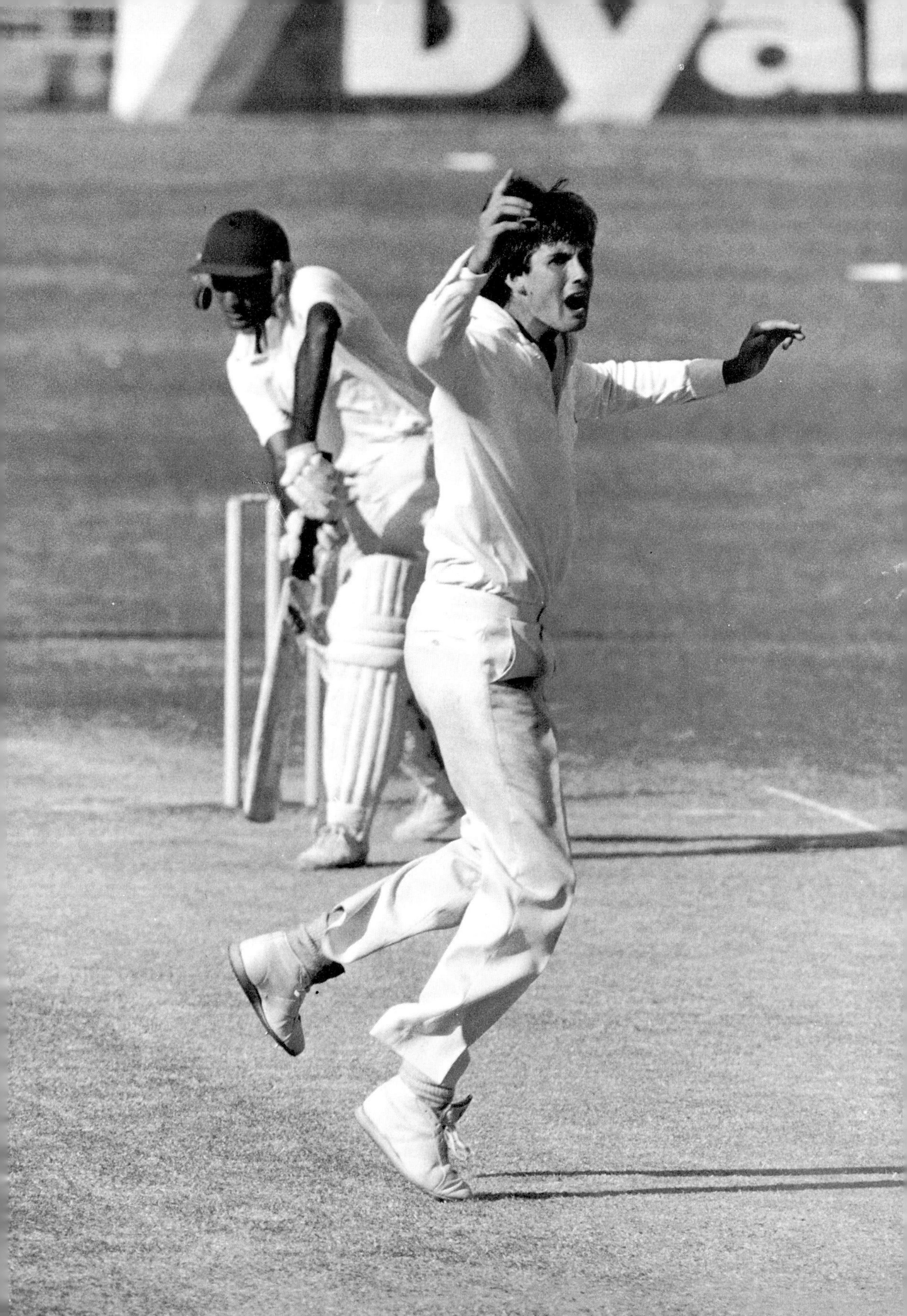

Above: Graeme Fowler 201. Mike Gatting 207. (*Adrian Murrell*)
Opposite: Neil Foster 11-163 (*Graham Morris*) . . . match-winning
performances in Madras

I fielded my heart out. If I come off a cricket ground feeling I've done that, whatever my other areas of failure, I've enjoyed the day. I may be covered in grass stains and mud, I may look untidy, but that is fielding. (Jim Swanton and I may disagree on this one.)

Even with Fowler and Gatting's double hundreds it was Foster's match. He dismissed Gavaskar twice, Vengsarkar twice, Amarnath twice, and five others. A man who had suffered considerable pain 'bent the back' which had given such trouble, and took eleven wickets in a vital Test match. He did everything right, we did everything right, and where better than in front of the chairman of selectors?

With the Fifth Test coming up at Kanpur, a bowler's graveyard, we had the series within our grasp. Surely we wouldn't let it all slip away from us now?

We didn't, and history had not repeated itself.

Celebrations after going 2-1 up in the series (*Graham Morris*)

FOURTH TEST MATCH
Madras, 13, 14, 15, 17, 18 January 1985
England won by 9 wickets

INDIA

*S. M. Gavaskar b Foster	17	c Gatting b Foster	3
K. Srikkanth c Downton b Cowans	0	c Cowdrey b Foster	16
D. B. Vengsarkar c Lamb b Foster	17	c Downton b Foster	2
M. Amarnath c Downton b Foster	78	c Cowans b Foster	95
M. Azharuddin b Cowdrey	48	c Gower b Pocock	105
R. J. Shastri c Downton b Foster	2	c Cowdrey b Edmonds	33
Kapil Dev c Cowans b Cowdrey	53	c Gatting b Cowans	49
†S. M. H. Kirmani not out	30	c Lamb b Edmonds	75
N. S. Yadav b Foster	2	c Downton b Cowans	5
L. Sivaramakrishnan c Cowdrey b Foster	13	lbw b Foster	5
Chetan Sharma c Lamb b Cowans	5	not out	17
Lb 3, Nb 4	7	B 1, Lb 4, Nb 2	7
Total	272	Total	412

1–17, 2–17, 3–45, 4–155, 5–167, 6–167, 7–241, 8–243, 9–263

1–7, 2–19, 3–22, 4–212, 5–259, 6–259, 7–341, 8–350, 9–361

	O	M	R	W		O	M	R	W
Cowans	12·5	3	39	2	Cowans	15	1	73	2
Foster	23	2	104	6	Foster	28	8	59	5
Edmonds	6	1	33	0	Edmonds	41·5	13	119	2
Cowdrey	19	1	65	2	Cowdrey	5	0	26	0
Pocock	7	1	28	0	Pocock	33	8	130	1

ENGLAND

G. Fowler c Kirmani b Kapil Dev	201	c Kirmani b Sivaramakrishnan	2
R. T. Robinson c Kirmani b Sivaramakrishnan	74	not out	21
M. W. Gatting c sub b Shastri	207	not out	10
A. J. Lamb b Amarnath	62		
P. H. Edmonds lbw b Shastri	36		
N. A. Foster b Amarnath	5		
*D. I. Gower b Kapil Dev	18		
C. S. Cowdrey not out	3		
†P. R. Downton not out	3		
P. I. Pocock did not bat			
N. G. Cowans did not bat			
B 7, Lb 19, Nb 17	43	Lb 1, W 1	2
Total (7 wkts dec)	652	Total (1 wkt)	35

1–178, 2–419, 3–563, 4–599, 5–604, 6–640, 7–646

1–7

	O	M	R	W		O	M	R	W
Kapil Dev	36	5	131	2	Kapil Dev	3	0	20	0
Chetan Sharma	18	0	95	0	Sivaramakrishnan	4	0	12	1
Sivaramakrishnan	44	6	145	1	Shastri	1	0	2	0
Yadav	23	4	76	0					
Shastri	42	7	143	2					
Amarnath	12	1	36	2					

### (v)	India: the press

By placing John Woodcock's paragraph at the beginning of this chapter on India I have acknowledged the accuracy and skill of top-quality reporting. But for a professional sportsman the relationship with the press can be a problem. Not in the obvious headline-grabbing nature of a row, but to have your game analysed, praised or more to the point criticised may be quite bearable when some considerable time has passed – it is not anywhere near so easy to swallow over breakfast the very next morning, with a hard day in the field ahead.

Each day you open the papers to see what they've said. You don't of course *have* to look; you can avert your eyes whenever you hear a paper being rattled open next to you, and some players seem to keep clear of all the irritation, but even if you don't read the report yourself you soon enough pick up the gist of it during dressing-room conversation, and sometimes you pick up completely the wrong angle.

'Have you seen what X wrote about you? Dear, oh dear!'

On tour it's different because you don't see the papers next day; you might only receive a garbled version from back home. Before and throughout the tour of India Jonathan combed the morning press to check how my performances were described. Below we have listed, without animosity and with a smile, a few of the more interesting comments. The quotes are not attributed but you might see a pattern emerging.

1.   Is his son good enough to follow him?
2.   The tour as a whole has had enough set backs, but Cowdrey has been a disaster within a disaster. He has played one match, scored eight runs and bowled four overs. Between while he has hobbled, sniffled, electrocuted himself and almost burnt a finger off.
3.   Cowdrey played unselfishly.
4.   For the first time Cowdrey looked to be in his depth.
5.   At times he made the ball fairly hum. If anything keeps Cowdrey in the Test side it will be his spirit.
6.   Cowdrey never looked convincing, but at least he got his head down.
7.   Cowdrey has the knack of taking useful wickets, an all-rounder with the right pedigree.
8.   Cowdrey played a succession of effective situation shots that his father could not possibly have taught him, including a sliced six over extra cover.

John Thicknesse of the *Evening Standard* and I playing backgammon on a day off. Paul Downton is the judge of fair play (*Patrick Eagar*)

9.   There is suddenly a striking resemblance from the distance between Cowdrey and a youngish Botham. They have the same strong build, the same prowl at the crease. A flat-batted six over extra cover, which Cowdrey hit off Kapil, was a formidably powerful stroke.
     (8 and 9 describe the same stroke!)
10. Cowdrey's effort in the field typified England's enthusiasm.
11. What he lacks is discipline, not punch.
12. It is not, I think, that he is incapable of bowling accurately, but rather that he has an irresistible desire to try to beat the bat. In his own interests it is time he tightened up his line and acquired, for use in these one-day games, a mean length.

Agnew, Ellison and Cowdrey. Moments of relaxation by the pool in Bangalore. It looks as if the curries have affected Aggers more than Elly and me! (*both Adrian Murrell*)

13.   Cowdrey will surely not play for England again.

14.   An amazing piece of fielding. Amarnath was so sure that his firm on-side push would pass well wide of Cowdrey at short leg that he set off, all unconcerned, on a run. Within a trice Cowdrey, with a diving save and reverse flick, had missed the batsman's wicket by a hair's breadth, with Amarnath far from home.

15.   It was always unlikely that he would be as good as Colin Cowdrey, who possessed a gift for games that bordered on genius.

And finally, this one is, I admit, by Vic Marks:

16.   In contrast to his father he's a gritty, down-to-earth cricketer who doesn't look very pretty.
(I'm beginning to worry about Victor.)

(vi)   India? An impression

But how can I give you a real sense of India, of travelling through it as a player? I can't. Perhaps the best I can do is gather together some phrases I jotted down, phrases that whirl around in my head when you ask me, as of course everyone did:

'What was India like, then?'

'Yes, your father, I knew him very well, please come in' – pack – travel – practice – play – eat – sleep – eat? – tummies – sweet and sour chicken – cyclists – curry – hot and sweaty gloves – short leg, knees ache – groin not great – team meetings – Taj Mahal – tiny taxis – dodgy food – dry state – dogs – struggling on the grog front – dogs – dust – 'Siva-who?' – sore throat – 'Siva-whatshisname' – chasing totals – cheating or error? – forged tickets – friendly faces – poverty – backgammon – dodgy water – mosquito

India 1984/5: a great experience (*Graham Morris*)

spray – pervading smells – 'Azza-who?' – Air India – Azza-Azza-Azharuddin – slow turners – fire crackers – rubbish dumps – drinks permit – bumpy bus to Poona – crowd roars – 'Good luck, Cow!' – cows – 'We can kill the cow here' – Cuttack – goats – Henry – ex-pats – bullocks – plush clubs – poverty – formal functions – 'It's a jacket and tie job, lads' – 'They're not going to give *that* out, I don't *believe* it!' – Chinese meals – Indian meals – Delhi belly – the lush trees and green grass of Gauhati – up country – up all night in the loo – I must see the funny side of the loo – insect killer – runs at last – forget the mosquitoes – what *is* the funny side of the loo? – hands on your arm – Bangalore, 'your father was born here' – 'Your autograph please, your good name, sir, please' – sleeping badly – Everest – Kapil's recklessness – throat aches – orange throwing – catches dropped – catches caught – appeals – Scotch in the team room – sucking Strepsils – Gymkhana Club – 'John Smith's bitter!' – swimming pool – sunhats hit the deck – '9.30 start? You're joking!' – players and press – class tells – people sleep in the street – lepers – leg spinners – 'We're behind the rate, 5.12, we need 5.2' – 'That smell, is it outside or in?' – shutters falling off hinges – hand-drawn carts – heavy cold – hot under helmet – Kent rang – bowling tight – beggars, 'please, please, I am poor' – luxury carpets – uneven bounce – Hyderabad rowing race – room-mates – 'Let's do it for everyone back home' – nets – snooker – letters – needle appeals – missing friends – tiny rooms – kitchen smells – scent of victory – losing weight but winning games winning games team spirit team spirit team spirit –

'Yes, your father, I knew him very well, please come in.'

5

In the spotlight? Australia

The nervy build-up to a big match, whether it's a prep school contest or appearing for Kent at Lord's or going out to do battle for England in Bombay, is all part of cricket's pressure, and it's the part spectators don't see. Before such an occasion your mental approach and practice and planning all need to be right. Different players need quite contrasting preparation for pre-season training or the Big Match.

If the TV ads and well marketed hype were to be believed, the series of One-day Internationals in Australia in February and March 1985 was 'The Greatest Show on Earth'. 'The World Series Cup' finished a few days before 'The World Championship' began. The 'product' was cricket.

All day my feet felt heavy. It was nothing to do with sadness at leaving India, nor anything to do with the excellent bottle of port placed in front of me somewhere between Delhi and Singapore. After some days off in Sydney, an exciting city I know very well, I had more or less recovered from three months of tiring and demanding travel and three hours of airline excess.

Yet my feet felt heavy, my body leaden. If I had to pin down the reason, without excuses, I'd say it was a kind of delayed lethargy, a psychological reaction to that release from discipline. In India we *had* to be self-controlled, we *had* to watch what we ate, we *had* to adjust carefully to a very different atmosphere. Relaxing with old friends in Sydney and tucking into more familiar food in superb restaurants, lying by a swimming pool, all seemed irresistible after Calcutta or Delhi belly. But by indulging ourselves so naturally in such comfort we lost that competitive hunger, and the tightly knit group identity. Both are difficult to achieve and once lost can be almost impossible to recover. Professionals should of course be able to relax and loosen up without losing their right frame of mind, yet somehow, deep down, we switched off. There are no excuses; it was a fact.

Certainly it wasn't over-confidence after our Indian victory. I tried hard to motivate myself, to prepare myself properly to compete amid the carnival, Big Deal atmosphere. I tried to move my feet and sharpen my mind, but it didn't work.

(i)   0 in Melbourne

When I looked out from my room in the Melbourne Hilton across to the massive bowl of the MCG, the crowds streaming along made the Nat West Final look a minor affair. In all, 85,000 turned up to see the lights turned on. Some of them wanted to see the cricket. Some simply wanted to have a go at us, and by the time we took the field for the Olympic-style parade the aggressive section was really in the mood. The Australian squad had a standing ovation all round. After their recent win in 'The World Series', the West Indies were received with great respect; the Sri Lankans with tolerant affection. We were booed and jeered all the way round the massive stadium, with an extra level of hissing from Bay 13. As expected, Bay 13 excelled itself with insults at David Gower and his men, making me think that if this was the Aussie crowd being normally aggressive at a major sporting event what were they like when they were abnormal? Some of the apples, for instance, came at a much faster pace than the Indian oranges at Bangalore. Most Indian throwers favour the gentle lob which lands over the top of the stumps. These Aussies had good arms and were going for direct hits at either end.

With the speeches (and then a few more) over we eventually got round to the cricket. David Gower won the toss against Australia and, aware of the problems of batting later under the lights, decided to bat first. Kitted out in blue, Fowler and Downton went in to face a white ball against a black sightscreen. The huge stadium was crammed.

The moment I want to concentrate on is not our impressive opening stand of 61 but the least impressive minute of England's

Part of the 85,000 crowd at the MCG (*Adrian Murrell*)

performance: my 'stay' at the crease. In the 39th over Lamb was caught off Lawson for 53, making England 159-4, which meant (batting at six) I had a ten-over innings to play. This is the kind of challenge I've often faced over the years and one which I particularly enjoy: improvise, nurdle, carve, nick, place or smash. Succeed and everyone says:

'Nice little cameo.'

Fail and everyone wonders why you played such a bad stroke.

'Good luck, Cow,' Neil Foster called, 'this is your kind of situation.'

It was the longest walk of my life. There cannot ever have been a wicket placed so far from the pavilion, and those 85,000 people were watching 'Young Cowdrey' walking out. While Lamb's hit was in the air, ending in Kerr's fine running catch, Gatting had crossed. He played the last ball of Lawson's over.

I took guard and looked round the field for gaps. There was a big space from mid-wicket to fine leg, an inviting space, a nice easy spot for a single or couple off the mark. Instead of remembering the simple basic advice of Richard Boddington at Wellesley – 'Watch the ball, Cowdrey, that's what you must do, watch the ball' – I was half looking for a gap on the leg-side.

I played across a ball from McDermott, first ball, and was lbw. Up went the finger, up went the roars. Oh no, wasn't it going down the leg-side? My father toured Australia six times (in 1954/5, 1958/9, 1962/3, 1965/6, 1970/1 and 1974/5) with immense success, winning friends everywhere. You have probably seen a photograph of the banner hung at the MCG, that tribute to him from his Australian fans. People still talk of his hundred in Melbourne on his first tour, and his highest first-class score, 307 at Adelaide. Six times he toured, being good enough at 20 and good enough at 40. On my big night I collected 0, first ball. Not good enough.

The walk back made the walk out seem extremely short. Accompanied by hoots and the visual aid of an electronic duck, I wanted to run, feeling I had knocked over the first fence at the jump-off. On the huge board the replay of the delivery went up and, to another big roar, I was lbw all over again. Then, just in case I hadn't fully grasped how bad everything was, I watched a duck waddle across the board, quack, quack, and drop a few electronic tears.

Out of the cauldron and into the warmth and security of the England dressing-room.

'How did that decision look?' I asked Paul Downton.

'Might just have clipped leg stump.'

This is a good response; a non-committal balanced reply stops you being unnecessarily irritated or indulging in pointless anger. Paul, one of my best friends, had as always found the most helpful way of dealing with the stresses of the game as they affect an individual sick with disappointment. By the end of the night the disappointment was general.

We made 214–8 and lost by seven wickets.

Even more disappointing to me personally, I didn't field well. On one occasion I failed to pick up the flight of the ball in the lights, although I helped run out Kim Hughes. There was an annoying heaviness about my whole performance, and I wasn't asked to bowl; this took away my final hope of redeeming myself.

The non-stop noise of that match is still with me now. Out in the middle it was extremely difficult to communicate with other members of the team, and without that contact it is a problem keeping the right spirit going.

Worse was to come.

You mean it can get worse?

Oh, easily.

Next match we went up to the old gold-rush town of Ballarat to play the Victoria State side. Unlike the bumpy bus ride to Poona this took only one and a half hours, but Mike Gatting was still with us and still with the same music. Since Poona he'd worked all through his tapes and was back to 'Private Dancer'.

This time I'm going to play naturally, I thought, I'm going to watch the ball. Either that or I'll hide Gatt's cassette player.

On a bouncy 'sporting' wicket in Ballarat I made 32, mostly off a mouth bowler who 'sledged' (abused) me after every shot. Then, after Robinson had cracked a thumb, I had my hand broken. I knew from the moment I was hit that the injury was the end of my involvement in Australia, and might even affect the beginning of the English season. All the cold numbing sprays in Bernard Thomas's big bag couldn't take away the pain or reduce the swelling.

Medical details are extremely boring unless you are afflicted with the very same problem. I'll assume my readers do not all have broken hands. Certainly the orthopaedic surgeon in Melbourne came briskly to the point. He grabbed hold of my hand. I jumped.

'There's no way you'll play for six weeks, mate.'

'Oh dear.'

'How's your Dad? I remember in . . . .'

So, for the build-up to my first season as captain of Kent, I would be in plaster: plaster for three to four weeks, going gently for four to five weeks, season starts in seven weeks.

Oh well, the break in my hand could have been worse, and there were joys to come before returning home: a meeting with Harold Larwood.

Harold Larwood, with M. C. Cowdrey and C. S. Cowdrey

(ii)   Listening to Larwood

I drove across the Sydney suburbs with my father, heading for Leonard Avenue, Kingsford. To be honest I've never been a great one for taking an interest in famous players of the past. The more recent past, say Sobers, yes, but like many current players I'm just a little sceptical of the old stories, how everything was done and usually done better in this or that day.

Harold Larwood (the real man, not the joke recently featured in the TV comedy serial *Bodyline*) is, however, another matter. I first met him about twenty years ago at the bungalow where he still lives with his wife Lois, and happily surrounded by children, grandchildren and great-grandchildren.

The scene is set in his home, about three miles from the Sydney Cricket Ground. Cowdrey M. C. and Cowdrey C. S. are warmly welcomed into his sitting-room. Mrs Larwood brings in a delicious tea (the sort of tea you had in the old days and definitely better than anything today!). The television is on quietly, for the cricket of course, but Harold's sight has almost gone now. He no longer can see the action on the screen so will have missed Cowdrey C. S.'s dismissal earlier in the week.

Cowdrey M. C. and Cowdrey C. S. listen, eat and ask questions. Harold, who is 80 and as lively as can be, still sounds a son of Nottingham. At 14 he was down the mine at Annersley Colliery and there's a strong, determined flavour to his talk.

He wags a finger at the TV screen.

LARWOOD: As for those pyjamas, I wouldn't have worn them in bed, let alone play cricket in them. Wouldn't have let my wife see me in them. And let me tell you, Jack Hobbs wouldn't either. Can you see Jack Hobbs in those blue things? Nor a helmet either. If I'd seen a batsman in a helmet I'd have bowled a yard or two faster. I'll tell you what, lad, you've just been to India, haven't you, well an Indian came in to bat at Nottingham once, came in wearing a turban at Trent Bridge, and I spent all the time trying to knock it off his head. True. Bad bowling, but true.

And I gather you're captaining Kent, young Christopher. Well, I'm going to give you a few captain's tips. Because I played with one of the best, Mr Jardine. You must look after your players. That's a good rule. And Mr Jardine was very keen to have his best players chaperoned, especially the night before a big day. In

Brisbane in 1933 we were given a rough time. And Mr Jardine called Bill Voce over and said: 'Now then, Bill,' he said, 'I want you to look after Harold. No drinking. Early to bed. And that's orders. Tomorrow's a big day.' That's what Mr Jardine said. So Bill Voce was my chaperon, was in charge of me you might say, and we had a very quiet meal in the hotel. Orange juice we drank. And then the telephone rang and some friends asked us over for a drink. 'No, sorry,' said Bill. Well, they said: 'Come on, just one.' Yes well, it's always the same old story, isn't it? We went and there was a big keg of ale. But no, I had another orange juice. Then just before we left I relented. Re-lented. That fatal first pint. And a pint for the road. OK. And just one more and we'll be off. Well, you know as well as I do we got out in a very good mood, singing and dancing. We *drained* that keg, we did. I wondered about my head in the morning. Well, we got back to bed about 1.30. And the next morning I was top pace, I can tell you. Shot out Bradman and Ponsford. Got four. At the end of the day Mr Jardine comes over to Bill Voce, 'Well done, Bill!' he said, 'You did well.'

Yes, young Christopher, you look after your players.

(He looks at TV.)

Pyjamas!

And be careful who you ask to be nightwatchman too. After bowling for hours I once got told by Mr Jardine to do that, to be nightwatchman. I'd bowled thirty-five overs! I was finished, I was furious to be asked to do that job. Anyway I was padded up. Five minutes to go and Mr Jardine glaring. Tremendous roar went up, and I was in. I was in a filthy mood, I don't mind telling you.

'Get your pads on, Les,' I said to Les Ames before I left, 'you'll be in next ball.'

Mr Jardine had no right to ask me, you see. And I'd made up my mind. If I hit the first ball I'd hit it straight at Bradman, he was the best fielder, and I'd run. Well I did hit it, *and* straight at Bradman, and I called Wally Hammond for a crazy single. Bradman had time, all the time in the world. I had to be out by yards. Well, Bradman throws it at the stumps. And just missed. Four overthrows. Larwood 5 not out. I was furious. Trying to get out first ball in a Test match and I'm 5 not out after one ball. I was in that filthy a mood.

Leslie Ames: a great man. He
celebrated his 80th birthday in 1985
(*Kent Messenger*)

Next morning I was still in a terrible temper. Well, Wally Hammond turned to me on the way out to bat and said: 'We could get a few here, Harold.' And do you know we batted through till lunch. To my surprise Wally got out. Before me. And then Maurice Leyland came in. Well, there was an off-spinner on, and I hit him for three fours. He was no problem, no problem at all. And Maurice came down the wicket and said:

'Have you seen the scoreboard, Harold?'

'No,' I said, 'what's wrong with it?'

'Nothing's wrong with it. You've got 98. Be careful.'

And so, next ball, with great caution, I half-hit a full toss carefully down mid-off's throat. 98. Out. I'll tell you what, that innings got me more friends and comments than seven years of bowling.

(Cowdrey, father and son, nodding and laughing.)

Yes, true that is.

Then there was my broken foot. At the Sydney Cricket Ground

this was, just over the way. This is to do with captaincy, young Christopher. I'd broken my foot but Mr Jardine wouldn't let me go off. He made me keep bowling. Woodfull and Bradman were in. I bowled off one pace. I couldn't bowl. Well, very generously, and I remember it to this day, Woodfull played them all, the whole over, gently back down the pitch to me. That was a good effort, very generous I thought. We had respect for each other in those days. They wouldn't do that today. Yes, that was a very good effort, that was.

The next over Bradman was out and Mr Jardine came over and said: 'You can leave the field now, Harold. If you'd gone off before, Bradman would have scored 400. We needed you on the field until Bradman was out.' So Bradman and I left the field together. Yes, Mr Jardine treated us as men. Men, not kids.

I mentioned Les Ames just now, and you're both Kent men. Have I told you about the only six I was ever hit for? Only one. Well, at Adelaide Mr Jardine and the others reckoned I wasn't bowling quick enough. I mean I was bowling quick, but not quick enough. *They* reckoned. Usually Mr Jardine got me going but he said nothing. Then at the end of an over he spoke to Les Ames - I found all this out later, you see, that Mr Jardine had told Les to gee me up a bit.

Next over Les comes up, tapping his keeper's gloves together, and says:

'What's going on?'

'What do you mean?' I said.

'What is this,' Les said, 'you're half pace.'

'Half pace!' I said.

'Yes, I thought you were a fast bowler.'

In fact he was quite rude to me as well, was Les. That got me mad. I turned and pointed to him and said:

'You just won't be allowed to forget that.'

I wasn't in a good mood at all, not in a good mood. Anyway I waited. I waited. I had to wait quite a bit. And in 1934 Kent came up to Notts, Trent Bridge, and the wicket was quick, it was quick I can tell you. D'you know, a lot of amateurs never played at Trent Bridge, year after year I waited for these amateurs, where were the amateurs I asked myself? I couldn't see them. But Les Ames was there of course and I was bowling!

Just before lunch I got a wicket which meant he had to come in. There were two balls left before lunch. Les took guard. And I called down the wicket,

'Adelaide.'

He looked at me. 'Sorry, didn't hear that.'

'Adelaide,' I said. 'Watch out, young man!'

And the first ball I bowled was a yorker, which is what I bowled mostly, I wasn't a bouncer bowler at all. A good yorker I bowled, but Les dug it out. Dug it out well. Anyway next ball, last ball before lunch, I gave him the lot, the quickest short one I could. But he was on the back foot, waiting wasn't he, and hooked me for six to the top seat of the stand. The only six I've ever been hit for in my life. Top of the stand!

We walked off, arm in arm, Les and me, laughing all the way.

Yes, Les Ames, great batsman and a great keeper, Les. Used to put steak inside his gloves. Softened up the gloves. It was all right in the morning but by three or four in the afternoon he was smelling a bit behind the stumps. And sometimes he used to put the steak in water overnight, keep it soft, for the next day as well. Yes, you could smell him clear by tea-time, I can tell you.

Time to go. The Cowdreys stand on the steps. Mr and Mrs Larwood and their grandson wave. The taxi carries away the visitors.

I may have got 0 in Melbourne and broken my wrist in Ballarat, but my trip to Australia was worthwhile. I'd listened to a legend.

(iii)   Australia: Jonathan Smith

When it came to Chris flying from India to Australia I didn't have to drag out the big *Times Atlas* again. I have lived there and know the country fairly well and feel it is second home. Give me an outline map and I can fill in the state capital cities and, for good measure, slap in Bendigo, Bordertown, Ballarat, Wagga Wagga and even, at a pinch, Tidbinilla. As for the Snowy Mountains, the Blue Mountains, the Barrier Reef, the Barossa Valley, no worries, and me, I always barrack for the 'Roos'. Yes, I may be a bit lost on India but as I lean out of bed on cold, dark winter mornings and tune in to matches from Melbourne or Adelaide or Brisbane, even if Blowers is talking, I have a strong recollection of the look, smell and atmosphere not to mention instant recall of the kind of comments flying around the outer.

In 1974 I was at the Melbourne Cricket Ground, where they hung the famous banner up for Colin Cowdrey on his sixth tour of Australia. He had, you remember, been flown out to join the side then being battered and maimed by Messrs Lillee and Thomson. Somewhere among the tens of thousands I found a seat, placed my collection of chilled cans by my feet, forever hoping I would pass muster as a local.

My cover was quickly tested by a bristly wino on my left who kept lashing the already bruised Brits with all manner of abuse. Now, few care more than I about the cause of English cricket but, all things considered, on this occasion I opted for silence. Then he leant heavily to the right, elbow out and all over me. I quietly helped him back to the vertical and he said:

'I hate the ... Poms, don't you?'

In reply I came up with a sort of ambiguous nod, a multipurpose job that should in the heat of the day have seen me through with a man threequarters gone. It didn't. It wasn't sufficiently clear reinforcement of his view of the United Kingdom representatives down under.

'Naa,' he went on, staring at my face. 'I mean I *really hate* them, know what I mean?'

I knew what he meant all right. This time I made a kind of muffled agreeing sound which didn't quite shape itself into a word, and looked desperately round for an alternative spot to settle, as a rabbit might with a fox in the paddock. There wasn't an inch for a pusillanimous Pom to run to. As a diversion I opened a can and took a long draw on the cool, amber liquid.

But how long could he keep up this one-sided conversation and how long could I escape detection? One word and I was finished, that was certain, but if I didn't speak at all perhaps the perception might eventually dawn on him that he was sitting next to an arrogant, stand-offish snob and that concept would for my neighbour tend to equal your average Pom, and there isn't a more average unit than that. Fortunately the sight of me drinking made him reach down for his bottle of red. He reached and reached a bit more and rolled in a slow relaxed way full off the seat and remained horizontal for the rest of the session.

He was smashed and so, on the field, were we.

While in Melbourne in 1974 Colin wasn't the only Cowdrey on my mind. I heard from Chris, a long letter from school with details of the early season results. He didn't say how he personally was doing, concentrating instead on the moves necessary to find the right team spirit and most effective combination. Bill Sale, his headmaster at Wellesley, told me Chris was always looking to encourage others, always batting or bowling as the situation required; not looking for ways of improving his average, but for ways of turning a draw into a win or a lost cause into a sensational victory.

It never occurred to me though, in 1974, that I would ever see Chris play for England in Australia, under floodlights, in blue kit, white helmet and with a big duck dreamt up by some electronics moron. If you had said all that to me in 1974 I would have raised a short scornful laugh.

'Leave it out, will you!'

But what will we be seeing in 1996?

I enjoy Australia. I love it. But I did not enjoy the 1985 'World Championship of Cricket'. And it isn't that we lost. No, along with Harold Larwood and most others I know, I can't stand the kit.

> CHRIS: Well, I don't agree with that for a start. I think it's quite fun – for a change. It adds a bit of colour, the blue shirts.
> JONATHAN: Typical Chelsea mentality.
> CHRIS: What's wrong with it? Did you watch it?
> JONATHAN: Yes of course I watched it but –
> CHRIS: Well, you can't have hated it that much. And I suppose you don't like the white ball either?
> JONATHAN: Well, you certainly found it hard to pick up.
> CHRIS: Look, how many Tests have you played?
> (FADE)

However, neither Chris nor I like the increasingly unpleasant racism, nor the cheap gimmicks. They contain nothing to attract people who care for cricket. While the quality of the TV camera work was slick, the amount of cricket shown on the screen was insufficient. Crude commercialism achieved overkill, a lot of fancy packaging but only a small gift inside.

As for the instant replays from all angles, even of a straight-forward catch at extra cover which even I might have caught, I found them time-consuming when more cricket, more of the true rhythm and ebb and flow, could easily have been shown. Much of the commentary was banal.

As a distinguished Australian Test cricketer said to me recently: 'When are we going to wake up? When are we going to see what we're doing to the game?'

6

1985

(i) Captain of Kent

1985 was a frustrating season for cricketers. It was an infuriating season for Kent. First, the weather. In between April and September I spent many hours explaining to friends, supporters, press and committees our feelings when our grounds are not blessed with fine or at least dry weather: the depression and gloom that tends to fill a dressing-room when, yet again, the dreaded drizzle and bad light had prevented any play. Worst of all, when this robs you of a good result it can – at a crucial stage – damage morale and you watch those high pre-season hopes drown in the damp scene before your eyes.

By July 1st nomination whist with Benson and Dilley had become monotonous. By August 1st Dilley could not afford to play any more. To keep the peace we gave Dilley a 70 point start. By September 1st Dilley had recouped. Elsewhere in the dressing-room bodies were sprawled: some sleeping, some listening to their Sony Walkmans, some reading, some staring at the rain and 'up to here' with their chosen profession. It's not easy getting the act together when the main message of the day is:

'There will be another inspection at . . . .' or 'Ladies and Gentlemen, we are very sorry . . .'

I looked out from the balcony. Under umbrellas or hidden away behind steamed-up windscreens, were the supporters who had driven many miles to see some play, to wait for some play, to listen to the announcements, to drive home. Eventually, however, all this weather chat seemed an excuse for failure. Didn't Ian McGaskill say it was raining everywhere else too?

Above: As so often, Nick Cook says it all! (*David Munden*)

Opposite above: Leading out Kent. Many people want to see the cap worn. Here it is!

Opposite below: Brian Fitch – our head groundsman spent most of the season on 'The Whale' (*Kentish Gazette*)

1985 was my first season as captain of Kent and the most important thing for a captain, especially a new one, is a good start. All eyes are ready to check on the new Cowdrey, all ready to compare results. It was particularly important for me as I had been appointed in September 1984, under what is politely called 'a slight cloud'.

Chris Tavaré had been deposed after leading us for two seasons (finishing seventh and fifth in the championship) and twice taking Kent to the Nat West Final. Under him, although we never quite threatened to lift the championship, we had been steady. Chris, a degree and blue from Oxford, a Test cricketer of proven ability, and a highly respected member of the Kent staff, was appointed as captain for 1983. I was his main rival for the post. In 1982, with Asif Iqbal in charge, Chris and I were made joint vice-captains, with the clear suggestion that he or I would ultimately take over. I didn't want to 'compete' while we were playing in the same side together and I didn't believe either of us would captain Kent with much conviction in those circumstances. But we both accepted the idea.

In the winter of 1982, following the retirement of Asif, Chris Tavaré was appointed skipper for 1983, and C. S. Cowdrey was invited to be vice-captain. Although disappointed I understood the decision. He was well qualified for the job. The main reason I had not been appointed was that I had not shown myself to be 'good enough' as a player. Not 'good enough'. My performances did not justify the captaincy of Kent County Cricket Club. The facts were put to me as clearly as I have put them here.

I was rather demoralised by this. I even considered whether I should continue any longer in the game, and if I did go on, perhaps it should be with another county? Nobody had ever told me before that I wasn't good enough and I sat through a long, depressing, thoughtful week in my flat in Neutral Bay, Sydney, where I was spending the winter playing for Cumberland Cricket Club in Parramatta. But that depressing, thoughtful week was necessary. It was a turning point. I came to realise that the Kent Committee was quite correct: I wasn't, on the evidence so far, good enough. There was some truth in this. I hadn't put in the hard graft on my game, and since being awarded my cap in 1979 my figures did not suggest I had made the right kind of progress.

During the next three months I worked on the many technical flaws in my batting. The winter months are the best time for English professionals to improve or revise their techniques, because once we become involved in the home season, the cricket and travel and benefit functions come so thick and fast there is little time for concentrated practice. All that winter in Parramatta I hit the ball straighter; I had to develop my off-side play. In recent seasons I had become very strong on the leg-side, but if the bowlers pitched outside the off-stump I was struggling. Robin

Jackman, for example, would rarely give me a straight ball that I could whip through mid-wicket or even past square leg. In Australia in 1982/3 I virtually blocked out the leg-side. While working on this change I didn't score that many runs, as often happens in a transitional phase, but week by week I could feel my game improving. It wasn't a matter of altering my grip or stance or anything major to look at. I simply needed to adjust my mental approach, my preparation for an innings. My pride had taken a knock and the knock spurred me to analyse my weaknesses.

With a new-found determination and growing confidence I returned for the 1983 season. I had a good start, striking a quick 100 against Cambridge at Fenner's, an innings which Derek Underwood is convinced was the major change in my career. I went on to have my best ever year, finishing with five centuries and placed as the second Englishman in the national averages, with 56·83.

My 1983 aggregate, combined with England selection for the tour of India 1984/5, was clearly enough to convince the Kent Committee I was now good enough. However I had not expected to be appointed captain, nor (may I add) had I in any way attempted to steal the job from Chris Tavaré. In every area and in every match I had tried to assist him for two years. But cricket is a cruel game at times, and in the same week that Chris Tavaré was left out of the England touring party to India he was 'relieved' of the Kent captaincy.

So, with considerable press interest in the change, I took over in 1985. What were the questions being asked in mid-April? Will the team back Cowdrey? Will Tavaré stay at Kent? Will there be a dressing-room split? Was it right to change the captain?

What will everyone be saying mid-June?

On June 18th 1985, we had just completed our eighth championship match. We had not won one. We were sixteenth in the championship (but top of the John Player Special League). It was hardly the start I'd hoped for, hardly impressive for a new captain in charge of a good side. From a personal, batting view, I had begun with a career best 159 against Surrey, with 95 in the second innings. I followed these scores with another 95 (v Middlesex) at Lord's. I have never had a better first few weeks. But from the team's point of view there wasn't much to cheer about – not only had we not won, to be honest we hadn't even come close enough to winning.

Hampshire needed three runs off the last ball to beat us in a finely balanced first match at Southampton, but we were accused of slowing the game down to deny them an extra over before the last twenty. In the next match I accused Surrey of being negative. Mike Gatting accused me of being negative in the next. On to Northampton where Geoff Cook apologised to me for not chasing 230 runs in 45 overs.

Accusations – complaints – apologies. But where were the results?

---

159 v Surrey at Canterbury. My career best score in the first home match of 1985 (*Kentish Gazette*)

Results came in the next three matches, all positive contests, all at home, but all were lost. When this pattern develops you tend to look to the one-day competitions and supporters start using phrases like 'salvage something'. In the Benson and Hedges we played very well to qualify, with extra luck on our side as we 'won' an unfinished quarter-final. That was the end of our luck. The semi-final was a miserable one. Mr Gower, whose world was now brightening by the hour, won the toss, quickly put us in and Leicestershire quickly bowled us out. As if this wasn't humiliating enough I injured my neck and so was unable to take the field.

'Oh dear,' said David, 'this isn't your day at all, is it!'

Determined enough? (*Tom Morris*)

Above: A nice moment for me in 1985. Younger brother Graham has just scored his maiden half-century for Kent v Australians at Canterbury (*Chris Cole*)

Opposite: Hit by Hadlee at Tunbridge Wells – a painful experience (*Patrick Eagar*)

'Sorry Jarvo, I should have caught that one.' (Please send alternative captions to the publisher!) (*Michael King*)

Not my month either, and I wasn't sorry to see the end of that section of the season.

A few weeks later ... transformation. We won four of the next five championship matches and out tumbled the cricket clichés. 'It's a funny old game' ... 'You might as well enjoy the good times' ... 'Things had to improve'. In a thrilling finish at Old Trafford – after I'd set Lancashire 260 in 59 overs – we won by 25 runs. Although Lancashire moved into a dominating position I kept up the attacking fields, took a catch I'm pleased to remember, and the luck rejoined us. 'County Cricket at its absorbing best,' Paul Fitzpatrick wrote in the *Guardian,* and we were applauded in by the home crowd who were fully aware that Kent risked losing to win. More success followed against Surrey and Yorkshire.

At Maidstone against Northants in mid-July cricket was suddenly not so much a cruel game as a rather silly one. At the end of the second day, after the other Kent bowlers had done all the hard work, I gave myself an over. The game was drifting. In a loose, gentle over I took wickets with my first, fifth and sixth ball. We were now in with a chance, and the next day took it. We played like a team who knew how to win.

16th ... 10th ... 7th ... 5th ... 4th in the championship table, and clear top of the John Player League by six points. 'Kent the team to watch' the headline said, and rain stopped us moving up to third. As if to confirm our new-found confidence we reached the quarter-final of the Nat West Trophy. Perhaps this would be our year? In the first round we chased a massive 296 to beat Surrey, and then quietly took care of the giant-killers, Durham.

Yet that victory against Minor County opposition was to be our last win in 1985. It is hard for me to believe the sentence I have just written. If I could explain it all it probably wouldn't have happened. It isn't good enough simply to shrug and say 'That's the way it goes'. You make it happen. We came close, of course, to winning other crucial matches, as close as 0·25 of a run in a rain-affected pocket-calculator JPL match against Yorkshire. And we lost narrowly – I'll never know how – to Essex, the eventual title winners, in the same competition. Again, at Eastbourne we were cruising to a big win over Sussex ... when those clouds zoomed in and rain dampened our resurgence of morale. You all know the sick, empty feeling when a victory is watered down into a draw.

Excuses, excuses, the same old story?

No, I think all that above is fair comment, but all counties could claim such fateful spells, and all captains must shoulder the responsibility when things don't go well. I am no exception. We played below our potential. We started to lose against less good sides, and I regret not being able to grip the problem. I regret not being able to turn the atmosphere and results around.

And I had further problems. Injuries. (Chris: Jonathan, are my injuries worth a chapter? Jonathan: Probably not. Perhaps a sentence or two.)

At Chelmsford, in the middle of one of my tidier spells, I was trying so hard to dismiss Graham Gooch, I pulled a side muscle.

Far from the glory of getting Gooch, I was sidelined and very sore for some weeks. Worse was to come. In the Canterbury Festival in August I caught a 'flu virus. I don't think I have ever missed a day of the Festival before, not one, always revelling in the holiday atmosphere, the large crowds, the tents encircling the ground, the bands, and the special feeling of belonging on England's most beautiful ground. In 1985 I was laid low and unable to help the side. The most I could manage was sitting muffled up and talking to my co-author.

Having dried up with excuses I take to heart Kent's disappointing conclusion to 1985. If I enjoy the praise when we win four out of five and when the headlines feature my captaincy, I must also take and accept the criticism. During my first season I learnt a great deal about all aspects of choosing and leading a team, both on and off the field.

I am optimistic about the future. There is plenty of reason to be.

(ii)   Richard Ellison
The big man on crutches bumped heavily into my front door. It hardly looked as if 1985 would be his year. Although he felt he had a reasonable chance of selection in the early season One-day Internationals against Australia, Richard Ellison knew the importance of first turning in some good performances for Kent. Although he had bowled well at times in India, he did not have much to show for it and the critics did not fail to point out his average. A steady First Test in Bombay, a little more swing in Delhi, and a quite remarkably courageous but unrewarded stint in Calcutta (0 to 117 in 53 overs) only led to his being omitted for Madras. Neil Foster came in, most successfully, and Richard left India, delighted for the side but a little disappointed with his own form.

A pensive Richard Ellison in early 1985, unaware of the great season he was about to have (*Adrian Murrell*)

In the Melbourne day/night showpiece he re-established himself with a spell of great skill and accuracy. Back home, however, waited a refreshed Ian Botham. Yet there was a realistic argument which found room for them both, especially as Richard's considerable potential with the bat had not yet been seen at international level.

However, on a slippery surface at Canterbury in pre-season nets, Richard fell heavily and badly sprained the ligaments in his ankle. As well as destroying any chance he had of playing for England in May, the fall was a major setback to Kent. Even when he resumed with the team, he was obviously not only short of middle practice but clearly suffering from the lack of pre-season training. (M.C. Cowdrey does not approve of all this modern pre-season build-up, but I do believe in the importance of hard physical preparation before the first match.) Anyway, after two weeks of watching Richard run in I was worried. To his displeasure I threatened to leave him out of the side for a while until he lost some weight and worked himself properly fit. He convinced me he would do this while still playing; and he was, as always, as good as his word. Within three weeks in June/July he lost nearly a stone. The wickets started to come – 'three for', 'six for' – and he moved swiftly up the first-class averages. A hard run on rest days, a big reduction in junk food, a wine and soda instead of a beer, and he was in top shape. 'I could murder a pint, Cow,' he often said, but he kept his aggression for the opposition and his will-power won.

Soon he was top of the averages.

His recall to the England team for the Fifth Test was no surprise to me. Yet it was not at all easy for Richard to be brought in at that crucial stage, with the series balanced at 1–1. The fifth, at Edgbaston, a ground with a history of County draws and Test Match results, was likely to be the 'crunch' contest. Richard had, however, two important advantages: first, he was bowling better and just a little quicker than ever before: secondly, he was still relatively unknown to the Aussies. In the day/night Melbourne game he bowled to Wessels, Kerr and Jones and the last two weren't even on the tour of England. Perhaps people had forgotten that opening spell under lights, 7–4–10–1, and remembered only Gatting's catch at slip?

After five days at Edgbaston the tourists would not easily forget either Allan Lamb's boot or Richard Ellison's movement in the air. In a year in which many bowlers had been arguing the ball was in fact swinging less, Richard 'made it talk', first this way, then that. Left-handers were in just as much trouble as right-handers and their top order included Wood, Wessels and Border, with Phillips to come.

In the most decisive selection I can remember Richard completely destroyed the Australians with match figures of 10-104. Perhaps more than anything, when no one had looked likely, day in day out, to dismiss Allan Border, Richard did so twice at Edgbaston and once more at the Oval. Prize wicket × 3.

> Border c Edmonds b Ellison 45
> Border   b Ellison 2
> Border c Botham   b Ellison 58

Tom Graveney said it was an 'eye-opener'.

How did he do it? All Tom needed to do was ask Alec Bedser or Fred Trueman. 'If you want to be a top bowler you've got to do something with the ball, line and length, around off-stump.' And that's what Elly did, to the excitement of thousands on the ground and millions round their radios and TVs. On the fourth evening he bowled five brisk overs and took four wickets for two runs. He reduced Australia from 32-1 to 36-5. Wessels, Wood, Holland and Border came and went, and that grinning bowler became a national figure. There's nothing like an Ashes contest to find England's new heroes. Has his analysis ever been bettered in a Test spell in recent years? Yes, by the man at second slip, the man who ran up to grip Ellison in that bear hug, the man who stands at second slip hands on knees but clings on to astonishing catches: I. T. Botham. He took 5-1 on the same ground in 1981. Ian took 5-1, Richard took 4-1. Most of us would settle for either.

Take me.

When Richard was getting another and another and another at Edgbaston, I was getting another and another as well. The last one, during the Test, was at Scarborough. The contrast was painful. I had failed to register for the third successive time in the County Championship, including my first ever 'pair'. I wrote a quick card and posted it to Birmingham.

Dear Elly

Congratulations on your fine performance. I am very pleased for you. I have just scored another 0. I was, though, very unlucky, because having played and missed at my first two deliveries I would have scored off my third, but second slip stopped it. Next ball I played back to a good length ball that pitched on middle and went straight on, and nasty Mr Oslear gave me out lbw. I will write again when I score a run. Keep up the good work.

Yours

Cow

Richard's friends now watched his life change. From back page in the averages, he and his moustache became front page on most dailies, some in bowling stride, some with Fiona, some drinking beer, some drinking champagne. The journalist's analysis was less of that superb high action, close to the stumps, movement both ways, and more on his thirst. The glass of wine was confirmed on breakfast television, but by the time the early edition of the *Evening Standard* was on the streets he was, our correspondent says, back on the beer. No, in the next photo it was champagne, the Gower favourite drop, as Richard won the Victoria Wine Cricketer Award. More bottles arrived. Instead of murdering a pint he was murdering a bottle of bubbly and making sure all around him were in on the slaughter. No one took all the fuss more naturally than Richard.

Elly captures the prize wicket of Allan Border again. This time at the Oval. It is good to see Ellison, Downton and Gower celebrating together. It had been a hard year for them all (*Adrian Murrell*)

In the curious way fixtures sometimes fall, after the Edgbaston Test the Australian bus headed down the M2 towards the St Lawrence Ground, Canterbury. The Kent match was their final preparation before the last Test. Richard, always popular with our home crowd, was by now into the folk hero category. Field a straight ball at mid-on and he was cheered to the echo; walk towards a section of the Woolley stand and the applause swept across the grass to meet him. In the dressing-room this development was not unnoticed. 'If he breaks wind after tea there'll be a standing ovation,' someone said. Richard led the laughter.

It was something of a dilemma for me as captain to know how much to bowl our front-page man. England wouldn't want him to be bowling lengthy spells at the Aussies, just in case they were able to find a last-minute solution to the problems he posed: it's often true (as with Sivaramakrishnan in India) that the more you face a new threat the quicker you work it out. However, my main loyalty was to Kent, who obviously wanted to beat the Aussies (and remember M. C. Cowdrey in Canterbury in 1975). Not surprisingly, knowing the English, we agreed on a compromise: I would not *over*-bowl him, but insisted that he should bowl whenever he was asked ... as if, being Richard, he would do anything less!

As at Edgbaston, the Aussies seemed totally bemused by him at Canterbury. First Hilditch, then Wellham, and he could have picked up three or four more, so consistently was he beating the bat or going through them.

Seven more wickets at the Oval and he had become one of the '85 Ashes All Stars, standing beside Gower, Gatting, Gooch – the G Force. In all this glory one moment stands out for me. In the evening I watched the highlights. To the second ball of the last morning, Border glanced Ellison. Paul Downton dived full length down the legside and nearly brought off a superb catch. As the ball spilled, instead of standing in critical disbelief Richard applauded the keeper's fine effort. In the next hour Paul took three catches. That said a lot, and was typical of both men.

Soon Richard's ticket was booked for the West Indies, and as the ideal build-up he married Fiona on 28 September. I was his best man and in my speech developed my long-held theory that his degree in PE from Exeter University was in Pie Eating.

Best man at Richard Ellison's wedding. In batting order: 1 Moxon,
2 Dyer, 3 Felton, 4 Lamb, 5 Cowdrey, 6 Johnson, 7 Downton,
8 Ellison, 9 Penn, 10 Foster, 11 Underwood, 12 G. Cowdrey (absent).
Scorer: Fiona. Spin may hold the key against Paul Downton's XI on
page 127 (*Robert Chapman*)

Nothing in my speech, however, equalled his opening: 'Ladies
and gentlemen, my job today is basically very simple. Like me
really.'

Richard, with his gentle nature, has frequently adopted this
rather faraway look. He enjoys the game of not being the quickest
wit around. In the Tonbridge School or Kent or England
dressing-room he will set it up, and soon earn the name 'Plank'.

'Why are you all calling me Plank?'

'Exactly, Richard.'

In his debut for Kent (against Hampshire) he was part of a big
tail-end partnership with Derek Underwood. During his 55 not
out Richard played an extra cover drive speeding towards the

Canterbury tree, speeding with such power the shot reminded Deadly of Sir Garfield Sobers. And even if it hadn't been quite that good a drive, Derek thought he'd encourage the young left-hander with the comparison.

'Sir Garfield, Elly.'

'Sir Garfield Who?'

Pie eating or soda drinking, setting us up for a laugh or bowling himself into the record books, Richard had a 1985 to remember. In a bad season for bowlers (wet run-ups, slippery ball, dodgy footholds and dead pitches), he became the first Englishman for seven years to head the national averages.

432·1, 113, 1118, 65, 17·20 are figures Richard will know and have every reason to recall with pride. Ellison's 1985 is a perfect illustration of the ups and downs of professional sport. Exhausted in Calcutta – with a 'wry, wistful smile' Vic Marks wrote – disappointed in Madras, on crutches in April, overweight in May, yet a genuine hero in September. His success in the last two Tests probably inspired the best in the England wicketkeeper who certainly became a busy man when that tantalising ball started wobbling first this way, then that. Richard, of course, knew his keeper well: they'd played together for Exeter University in the side which won the UAU title in 1979.

(iii)   Paul Downton

Like many players I find press vendettas hard to take. Perhaps the press don't see their stories and angles that way but they can be ill-informed and particularly hurtful. Take the case of David Gower. After his indifferent batting form in India and his slow start to the 1985 season he was all but written off by some of the press. A hundred against the Aussies in the third One-day International kept them quiet for a while and by the end of the Ashes contest he was once again a firm favourite. Which left Paul Downton. As we returned from India the knives were already being pulled out and sharpened. All summer they were waiting and by the last two Tests the knives were glinting in whatever sunshine filtered through.

Best man at Paul Downton's wedding. A good team, but it was a shame Edmonds and Emburey could not make it. In batting order: 1 Fowler, 2 Slack, 3 Gatting, 4 Gower, 5 Lamb, 6 Radley, 7 Cowdrey, 8 Downton, 9 Ellison, 10 Cowans, 11 Daniel, 12 Nicholas (for disciplinary reasons!). Scorer: Alison (*Graham Morris*)

Paul has been a close friend since we did battle against each other at school. I was also his best man on 19 October 1985 when he married Alison Naylor. For over ten years now I've played with or against him.

Sevenoaks is just up the road from Tonbridge. In the early seventies Sevenoaks School 'had' Tavaré, Graham-Brown and Downton; Tonbridge School 'had' Kemp, Cowdrey and a young Ellison. As Paul's opposite number at full-back in rugby I saw far too much of his quick, well-timed darts into the line, either creating an overlap or simply weaving elusively through on his own speed. With his instinct of what to do and the exact moment to do it, he usually left me standing. There was nothing flashy about his performance, there never is, but he was balanced at the right second and I didn't tackle him the whole afternoon. Sevenoaks 22, Tonbridge 8. Mike Gatting, his County skipper, reckons Paul is the best runner of twos he has ever seen in one-day cricket (and Gatt's not too bad himself between the wickets!). Paul's speed is also a great asset when keeping in a one-day game: without slips you have to cover a much wider area.

Still, whatever happened in rugby, Tonbridge had the upper hand in cricket, never having lost to Sevenoaks before (or since). In May 1975 with Nick Kemp ('The fastest bowler in the school-boy game') spearheading our attack and R. Ellison ('a promising colt') we were strong. After scoring 177-2 in quick time I declared early, fearing Sevenoaks would go for their let's-get-a-point-at-Anfield approach. They did, but a Tonbridge victory looked a formality, when Downton, on 10, snicked Cowdrey to Kemp at first slip. I hate to bring this incident up in front of old friends, and particularly when it means reminding none other than Nick Kemp of this, but ...

Peter Smith of the *Daily Mail* and I discuss cricket at the wedding!
(*Graham Morris*)

In-and-out, dear oh dear ... I don't believe it ... down it went. And Downton went on and on. At the other end, one by one, they yielded to the pressure of Nick Kemp's speed, but Sevenoaks somehow finished on 145–8, with Downton 96 not out. Yes, they'd got their draw, but more interestingly we had seen the future England wicketkeeper/batsman. In that rearguard action he revealed his quiet dedication, that well-applied technique in an innings unusual for someone still at school. (Strangely, looking at the scorebook, I see I didn't give Richard Ellison a bowl that day!)

Alan Dixon, the fine Kent all-rounder of the 60s, was the Tonbridge School coach that year, and saw three of us (Downton, Kemp and Cowdrey) picked for the Young England tour of the West Indies – Paul was my vice-captain – and soon we were all on contracts for Kent. It was also Alan Dixon who taught Richard Ellison how to swing the ball.

Paul and I were always room-mates. We travelled everywhere together, both batted down the order, and both played golf on our days off. We played cricket together in Australia, South Africa and in the West Indies. We met up in Sydney; we shared a house in Rondebosch. In South Africa we played golf each week against Gooch and Emburey. On the course Paul was called 'Steady Eddy'. He was always reliable either hitting a ball or preparing a barbecue, as patient and dedicated with the tongs and as persistent in getting the fire going as he was that May day for Sevenoaks. In comparison I was slapdash. (Knowing my tendency to serve meat burnt or raw, he told me quietly to keep to what I was best at – looking after the bar.)

In 1977/8 Paul was selected to tour Pakistan, as reserve to Bob Taylor. He had as little opportunity to shine then as Bruce French, who understudied to Paul, in India 1984/5, but by the end of 1979 he was awarded his Kent County cap. In so far as any cricketer has an assured future Paul's at Kent seemed clear ahead with the probable England place when Bob Taylor retired.

'After Packer', and after some speculation, Alan Knott now reconsidered his retirement. He signed a new four-year contract with Kent. Paul, aged 20 and no doubt expecting Kent to embark on a youth policy, immediately accepted this decision and asked to be released. Within days he was in demand from many Counties, and for obvious reasons went to Middlesex. Look at the benefits: Mike Brearley's captaincy, keeping to Daniel, Emburey and Edmonds, and all this at Lord's, with the extra exposure which often leads to an England selection.

For many the chance of joining Middlesex would have been a straightforward decision but Paul and I discussed it at considerable length, because Ian Gould, the Middlesex keeper, had toured with us both to the West Indies. Professional sport or not, Paul had no wish to push Ian out of a job. I was soon watching a vicious circle in which a group of fine keepers, all of whom I knew well, were affecting each other. Alan Knott felt bad about Paul leaving Kent; Paul was feeling bad at the prospect of taking Ian Gould's place at Middlesex. And, seeing it all coming, Ian Gould was just feeling bad!

Eventually Ian went to Sussex (where, I suppose, someone else felt bad) and Paul settled in to take Phil Edmonds and John Emburey. Keeping to spin is the big test and he would have Phil Edmonds tempting the batsman to drive, while John Emburey preferred to pin the batsmen down as tightly as possible. Then, when the quickies came back, Wayne Daniel would be bouncing high or skidding through, testing your reactions to top pace.

As we predicted, from Middlesex came his England place. All seemed rosy, but some moments are never forgotten and one came for Paul in 1981. Quite rightly he was picked for England against Australia for the First Test at Trent Bridge. There Paul dropped Allan Border, a simple catch, and was promptly dropped himself. In came Bob Taylor. He was dropped. In came Alan Knott.

Yet, so consistent was Paul over the seasons, week in week out, I expected all the talk to end when Taylor retired. Paul played all five Tests against the West Indies in 1984, and came out with as much credit as anyone.

Indeed his accomplished batting enhanced his reputation as a person of cool courage and calm technique under fire. Both as a middle-order man or make-shift opener he looked the part; he has made vital runs against Australia, the West Indies and India.

For the Indian tour he was the undisputed choice. But India poses its own special problems for keepers because the majority of wickets there keep very low, increasing the difficulty of timing your take. Even the very great keepers (Knott and Taylor) found it a special challenge to be consistent, with the unpredictable difference in bounce and turn. From short leg I noticed how often the ball went through ankle high or shot along the ground down the legside, sometimes scurrying off Paul's outstretched boot for byes to fine leg. Those hours I spent under the helmet, close to the action, crouched waiting, made me realise just what the keeper's problems were. It may all look easy on TV when you see one ball delivered and the keeper's error.

Paul is a perfectionist and judges himself by the highest standards (and there aren't any higher than his two predecessors), but on our return from India the hatchets began to whistle. Look at Gower's aggregate; look at Ellison's strike rate; Downton isn't as good as Knott (who said he was?). It was, I felt, only a matter of time before the vultures swooped.

(Jonathan: Knives, hatchets, vultures, watch the metaphors, Chris.

Chris: Oh, I was rather enjoying those.)

Anyway, Paul kept well at Headingley and at Trent Bridge. Once more he began to look secure in the side. But at Old Trafford ... With the series 1-1 and England desperately keen to capture the last five Australian wickets for victory on the final day, the very thing happened most keepers most dread: the top batsman, Allan Border (again!) played forward in Ian Botham's first spell, got an inside edge, Paul dived full to his right, and ...

You could hear the intake of breath from the television commentators.

Above: Downton – the wicketkeeper. He didn't allow the criticism to affect him

Below: Downton – the batsman. He has played several important innings for England (*both Adrian Murrell*)

Botham, Robinson, Lamb, Gatting and Emburey seem pleased with this catch of Paul Downton's (*Graham Morris*)

It was a very difficult chance, but the vultures flapped their wings, left those perches high up in the stands and began to circle the ground. 'One thing is for sure, Alan Knott would have caught it, no doubt about it, definitely.' The irony of dropping Border twice was too much.

The press demanded Knott's return, whether he ever intended to tour or not, never mind the future, get Knotty back. Now! Paul and I, all of us involved in cricket, knew Alan Knott was of course in excellent form, but I felt it would be a backward step to ask Alan to return, especially as he was on the verge of retirement.

Paul kept his place, which I considered the right decision for the present and the future. He was rightfully on the balcony with the others. Photographs in the papers don't easily convey the quiet, unobtrusively skilful job he does; there aren't any Downton war dances or flamboyant celebrations of what he has just achieved. It is not in his nature. But we all know he is a fine keeper and we especially enjoyed his catch to dismiss Kepler Wessels at the Oval (*not* a favourite ground for most keepers). Having caught it, he stood up and quietly got on with the game.

He's Paul Downton, 'Steady Eddy', not Bruce Grobbelaar.

(iv)   Caught Knott bowled Underwood

I have often enjoyed trying to predict the unpredictable genius of Alan Knott. Standing at slip, cover or mid-wicket, day after day for nine seasons, speculating what Knotty would do next, was a game at which I gradually improved. What he did was often likely to be either totally safe or extraordinary or both. With his batting, however, I became quite accurate, working on the basis that he'd do what no ordinary man would consider. I remember sitting (full of 'flu) next to Jonathan during the Canterbury Festival in 1985. Alan Knott walked in to face Norman Gifford. A very good moment was in prospect: a couple of exceptionally experienced players, a wily old bird bowling to the world's greatest wicketkeeper/batsman; a left-arm spinner turning the ball away from the bat of a man who keeps to the world's greatest left-arm spinner.

'What'll Knotty do?' Jonathan asked.

'First ball will be on or outside off stump,' I reckoned, 'and he'll sweep it fine.'

Norman Gifford duly delivered. Alan Knott duly obliged. Jonathan lowered his binoculars.

'Amazing! What next?'

Scores of times, of course, I've been wrong, but on one thing above all in his career I would have bet everything. That when he came to call it a day there would be no Knotty announcement of a final match, no chance for a big press turnout, no walk back in front of a full house standing ovation, no hope of a last lingering look at the little phenomenon whose career tally was:

18,105 runs (average 29·63)
1,344 victims (133 stumped)
95 Tests (how many more if Packer and South Africa ...?)
4,389 Test runs (average 32·75. Five centuries)
269 Test victims

No, I knew Alan Knott would somehow just not be there any more behind the stumps.

And so it proved in 1985.

During the summer, in which he had kept supremely and been often talked of in terms of yet another England recall, the ankle injury which had ruled him out of the 1984 Nat West Final returned. After 22 years at Kent he felt unable to go on, unable to go on at the exceptional level he always expected of himself. It was a sad day when I announced his retirement to the rest of the team. What was everyone thinking, especially Derek Underwood?

I often went to Canterbury as a boy with my shorts and long socks in 1965 to watch Knott and Underwood. Twenty years later I was captain of a Kent team which included them both, and I was well aware that their captain for a decade was M. C. Cowdrey. *Me* captain Knotty and Underwood! It must have felt equally strange for them.

Behind that little account of Alan facing Norman Gifford lies, of course, his uncanny ability to make extremely difficult things look so easy. Is that the definition of sporting genius? On the rare occasions when he did drop a catch it was perhaps almost comforting – he was human after all, even he could make a mistake. When he stood back to the pace bowlers it was hard to picture him dropping anything, and standing up to Derek Underwood was of course a sight all cricket lovers relished. For Kent it has been a privilege.

Alan's critics sometimes said he didn't stand up enough to medium-pacers. Knotty could do it as well as or better than anyone, but he believed too many catches (especially in one-day cricket) were missed that way. Given that the modern batsman tends to run the ball down to third man off an angled face, the edges tend to be very thick, much reducing the wicketkeeper's chance of taking a clean catch. How often we can all remember him standing back, anticipating, and leaping out far to his right, with no slip, and rolling over with the ball. Remember that quarter-final catch at Taunton in 1984, M. Crowe c Knott b Alderman? That catch could be the one which took us to the final. At times Bob Woolmer or I would ask him to stand up to our medium-pacers to put extra pressure on the batsman. If asked Alan would never refuse. Furthermore his performance would be faultless.

Whatever the arguments in Derby or Kent over the different gifts and methods of Alan Knott and Bob Taylor, Alan's batting clearly gave him the edge – even though a Knott coaching manual could well hospitalise a few and force many more into early retirement! One of his more unusual yet completely logical preparations was the way he batted in various styles. For a few minutes or so in pre-season nets he may practise as if for a championship innings. Everything would be careful and calculated to occupy the crease. After a while he would be satisfied with that. Then he would switch to a cup-tie situation, improvising a wonderful mixture of impudent strokes. Right, next comes Sunday afternoon and we've got to produce something incredible. For a few more minutes he would despatch the off-spinners, turning into the bat, through or over the offside field. When batting in these styles, although always Alan Knott, he would seem a different player in each. Even in 1985, when going in very low down the order, he played an unforgettable innings at Northampton. The wicket was seaming. We had collapsed to 120-8. For his first fifty he met the ball with a stroke as straight as the MCC manual; then suddenly he played every kind of game with the bowlers. He even amused Roger Harper who'd never seen anything like it. Knotty broke all the rules (except 'watch the ball') and enabled me to declare, A. P. E. Knott 87 not out. Right to the end of his career he could have batted in the top five and scored a thousand runs; but the constant strain of keeping in County cricket made him content to bat wherever he was placed. He was completely unselfish.

Linked with his innings, whether against Holding and Marshall or against Benson and Taylor in the nets, would be a Knott theory or plan, sometimes so eccentric by any cricketing standards that he was laughed at – or perhaps we simply failed to understand?

Because although a reserved man who loves family life, Alan was far from quiet in the dressing-room; there he kept the team going with all the 'incredible' events in a day in the life of A. P. E. Knott.

First his arrival; that was a business in itself. He arrived on a match day with so many bags and cases you thought he had unexpectedly accepted a four-month winter tour. Stepping carefully out of the car he would find some eager young kids waiting to transport his equipment to the dressing-room.

The car? Not a sponsored Saab or smart Japanese job with his name splashed all over the side. No, his car is a very special L registration Volvo, the most comfortable car he has ever had and one he will never take to the Herne Bay scrap heap. Comfort is essential. Of course a big block like the head of a croquet-mallet had to be fixed to the accelerator, thus reducing the movement of his legs (imagine pulling a hamstring going down the motorway . . . it could happen).

Having arrived safely at Canterbury he checked his watch. The estimated time of arrival varied depending on the many strange occurrences that only happened to the man in the L registration Volvo on the road from Herne Bay. An incredible storm, and then the newly laid roadworks erected seconds before he came along ('I can't believe it'). On most days the weather at the County ground was completely different from the sky when he left home twenty miles away. What had happened?

If the opposition won the toss and elected to bat first on a perfect wicket, Alan would be astonished: 'Batting first on this wicket? I can't believe it.' For the first hour he would stare into the cloudless sky in disbelief: 'Francis on Breakfast TV said it was going to rain.' So where *was* the rain?

Lunch was another hurdle. While we tucked into all three courses to help us through the next session, Knotty used every minute to the full. First, a complete change of clothing; the wet gear must go meticulously into the drying room; then make sure he was dry himself before putting on the fresh kit. When and only when all this was done could he think about settling down not to three courses but to a cheese roll with a slice of cucumber or tomato and a pot of tea. Not any old cup of tea but 50 per cent milk and cold water added if too strong, and sweetened (if at all possible) with Rumanian honey. Such details were important.

After 35 minutes, when the five-minute bell rings, he can never believe it.

'Is that the bell?'

A last mouthful, a quick sip, a hurried search for his handkerchief that must be hanging out of his left-hand pocket, just so, a final plea to the lads: 'Don't go without me, I'm sure the bell went early' and the best keeper any of us had ever seen was trotting out with the team.

On the field Alan was totally dedicated to the job in hand, keyed up in readiness for every ball, whether the game was a big decisive semi-final or the second day of a County match when things had gone more than a little flat. Sustaining concentration for a keeper is the main problem. Yet, by talking to slip and doing his famous exercises, he kept his mind and body supple and alert for anything that might happen, and even on the last ball of a dreary session he could suddenly leap up, springing right up, with mobility that suggested he was high on adrenalin all through the two hours. Another dismissal, a little jog of pleasure, the familiar, impish grin.

If forty minutes at the lunch interval wasn't enough for Knotty to prepare himself, imagine the problem of a twenty-minute tea break.

'The umpires aren't going out already? Don't go yet, Cow.'

In those last sessions (his favourite because it *is* the last), I often admired him most, collecting legside takes, always tidying up everything, and keeping to the highest standards. Good day or bad day for Kent, at the close of play Knotty would be content to sip a sherry and lemonade. Just one. Relaxing for the first time since 10 o'clock in the morning, he sat with a single sherry, the pint glass filled up with lemonade. On that bad day for Kent he will lift everyone with a humorous comment or two.

From fitness training to match preparation to helping others Alan Knott was a top professional. Afterwards was his time for quiet reflection with those who had taken part, not for drinking in a sponsor's box or surrounded in a nearby pub. Most important for him was the slow 'wind down' from the intense involvement of the contest; then a long shower and a complete rest, remaining a full hour, sometimes a little more, after the game. Then he would finally head off for Herne Bay (sudden shower of rain and roadworks permitting) for the best part of his day, a quiet family evening with Jan and James.

After I had announced his retirement to the players he stayed in the pub until nearly closing time. Unheard of! Especially important to me were his kind words for good fortune in the future, and his hope to stay in cricket in some capacity, coaching young wicketkeepers.

Caught Knott bowled Underwood (*John Turner*)

Alan Knott. He was meticulous about his clothing and equipment.
  I asked him if we could get dressed with him:

1 BACK-FLANNEL: 'Looking after your back is a very important part of
a wicketkeeper's career. Jack Jennings, the England physio in 1968,
first gave me the idea of wearing a back-flannel to keep my back warm
and soak up the sweat. In 1970 I tried without it in Madras and I got
a stiff back, so I have worn one ever since.'

2 SHIRT: 'It was vital that it wasn't tight across the shoulders, so I
always wore a very big shirt. I would wear a long sleeve to protect my
elbows when diving. But I had to take the buttons off the cuffs because
they would be too tight around my wrist. I just taped them up with
elastoplast.'

3 TROUSERS: 'The old baggy trousers for me. These nylon tracksuit trousers that a lot of keepers like nowadays make you sweat too much.'

4 BOOTS: 'I always reinforced the heels of my boots to give me extra protection on long days in the field. On the 1976/7 tour of India I tried rubber-soled boots for comfort, but I failed to get to a top-edged hook from Sunil Gavaskar, which I would have reached with studs on. John Lever, the bowler, was furious and I have never done it again.'

5 PADS: 'Most pads have three straps, but I found the middle one very uncomfortable for my calf muscles, so I removed it. Instead, I attached a big bandage around my leg and the pad to keep it secure. However, I had two straps around the bottom. I used to suffer from Achilles tendon trouble, so with two straps I could loosen one sometimes to ease the Achilles, but still keep the pad fastened with the other.'

6 GLOVES: 'I always liked an old, well broken-in pair of gloves. Despite you lot having a go at me all the time for looking scruffy, they were very comfortable, which is the most important thing.'

7 HANDKERCHIEF: 'Everyone thought it was a superstition to have my handkerchief hanging out of my pocket all the time. But it is very difficult to get it out with inner gloves on unless it was sticking out. The reason it was always my left pocket was because my left glove was looser and easier to get off.'

    C.S.C: 'Why was it looser?'
    Knotty: 'I don't know.'

8 HAT: 'It is very important for a wicketkeeper to have a heavy hat. Not only for keeping it on in the wind, but also when diving for a catch. I used to have a very good one from Miami made of sail-cloth, but for the last ten years I have worn one that Fred Titmus gave me in the West Indies in 1974/5. When it wore out, I tore up an old white shirt and Joan Taylor would sew it on to the hat, which would keep it heavy.'

    Knotty: 'Do you want to hear about my batting equipment?'
    C.S.C: 'I'll come back to you on that one, Knotty!'

I thought of Derek Underwood, losing his great companion. Kent has been lucky since May 1963 when, under 18, Derek followed Alan into the side and was soon the youngest bowler ever to take 100 wickets in a season. Lillee and Thomson, McEnroe and Fleming, Tom and Jerry, Laurel and Hardy, Torvill and Dean, Simon and Garfunkel, Rogers and Hammerstein, and in the Hop County, Knott and Underwood. Derek strides purposefully into the dressing-room, immaculately dressed in Kent blazer and tie and the trousers he wore for his first benefit in 1975. (And *don't* forget his 1986 benefit.) Having somehow avoided those storms and roadworks, there isn't a hair out of place – though that is becoming less of a problem these days, after all those overs into the wind in every part of the cricketing world.

'Sorry, I'm late.'

Derek puts down his kit bag.

The family had to prepare the picnic lunch, and the boiled eggs weren't ready, and there wasn't room for his kit, but he's straight out into a net for a practice bowl. For practice Derek walks out to bowl not in a tracksuit or training kit but smartly clad in the kit he'll wear all day. That's the way he's always done it, and there's little reason to change now. He couldn't change, any more than he could alter the flat-footed walk and the boots which seem more suited to climbing Everest than running through 25 overs.

'Morning mateys', and he's bowling his looseners and ready for the fray; he can't wait to get a bowl ('you can't take wickets unless you bowl'). Because Deadly's idea of a good day is 35 overs, 5 wickets for 70 (or less), a day of very hard work, determination, a bucket of sweat and a fair, just, return at the end of play.

On a belter (=a very good wicket) he will bowl tight, meanly, accurately, proving his theory that bowling is a 'low mentality profession: plug away, line and length, until there's a mistake.'

On a turner (=a wicket taking spin) he becomes very hard to keep out, and fielders like myself close to the bat can expect a sharp catch at any time.

On a 'bunsen' (=a wicket that explodes through the top surface) he is often unplayable.

On a 'wetty' (=a rain-affected pitch) no helmet, chest-pad, arm guard or Duncan Fearnley Magnum bat can save the batsman. The bowler is Deadly.

In 1968 I was taken to the Oval for the final day's play against Australia. My father was captain of England and the nanny who was with me had no desire whatsoever to be at the Kennington Oval with a young cricket-mad boy, especially as it was raining. She threatened to take me home. I burst into tears. She gave in. In mid-afternoon, with her mood more than hellish, the game eventually got going, and the wait was worthwhile.

England had little time left to bowl Australia out, and the determined John Inverarity was holding the baggy greens together. But it was a 'wetty' and, as expected, Derek bowled magnificently. With minutes remaining and Australia now nine wickets down, Nanny suddenly leapt out of her seat yelling:

'Come on, Deadly!'

It was the end of a remarkably determined innings by John Inverarity, who later taught at Tonbridge School in 1976/7 and went on to be the highest run-getter of all time in Sheffield Shield cricket. Although not one of Invers's major scores I am sure that Oval knock would rank high amongst the memories of one of Australia's most impressive men.

Anyway, back to Nanny. She was ecstatic. She was a convert. Most of us always have been and, seventeen years later, as Derek's captain in 1985, I found him more than eager to help with any of my problems. Offering him advice is not so easy because no one else has ever been able to bowl medium-pace spinners, controlling length, line and variation of pace at that speed. With a full glass and a packet of Benson and Hedges though, he will talk cricket for hours, enjoying his pints like a man who has earned them.

No, the strain isn't telling. Just a familiar expression from 'Deadly' during a long spell (*Adrian Murrell*)

On one occasion last summer, even though he and Graham Johnson had brought us our first championship win of the season at Old Trafford, he was far from pleased. His figures were 2–93 off 20 overs. There was no doubt who was to blame for that unusual Underwood analysis. I was. I asked him to chuck the ball up, to keep Lancashire and Jack Simmons in the hunt. Sometimes he was bowling with five or six men round the bat and disappearing for 10 or 12 an over. We needed Lancashire in with a hope of victory, so giving ourselves a chance too. As it happened, the gamble worked and Kent won with eight balls left. Derek was not purring.

When we arrived in Chelmsford late that night we had a long, detailed and constructive talk about why I felt he had to give so many runs away. Derek was understandably disappointed; he wasn't made to give easy runs to batsmen. That was not the way he treated batsmen, and not the way he believed a bowler should bowl. At the end, as we moved off to our rooms, we may not have been in complete agreement but his parting words to me summed up all I want to say about this remarkable cricketer.

'Whatever happened today is history. I'll back you all the way tomorrow against Essex. Let's forget it.' And I knew he would.

Without Alan Knott, he will be vital to us in 1986, and he deserves the best benefit Kent can bring.

(v)   Bowling to Botham

Although smaller and not as beautiful as Canterbury or Worcester, the County Ground at Taunton has an immediate appeal. You've probably seen it on TV as the venue for an exciting Sunday or knock-out competition. At one end the Quantock Hills, at the other those two towers, the towers of St James's and St Mary's churches. When I first played at Taunton there used to be a greyhound track and lighting around the boundary, reminding me as I fielded that if I failed in everything else I still had a chance on the dogs.

But the view of the hills and the dominant spires, and your memory of the dog track can quickly be spoiled if you are bowling to Ian Botham, especially if it is 1985 and you take the wicket which brings him to the crease.

He comes to the crease in a mood determined to rearrange matters, to 'change the complexion of the game', as the commentators are fond of saying.

On Tuesday 14 May 1985 this happened during a Benson and Hedges cup tie. Kent had built the highest score they'd ever made in the competition, 293-6, with Chris Tavaré scoring a magnificent 143. In reply Somerset were struggling, even against my bowling. After three overs of my spell I dismissed their opener, Julian Wyatt, for 22.

I had bowled three overs for four runs. Just the job.

Enter I. T. Botham, turbocharged, with respray on top.

I had bowled four overs for 22 runs. Only 18 off that over. (He was playing himself in.)

I had bowled five overs for 37 runs. 15 off that over, getting better.

All round the small ground I was blasted. I watched the ball soar towards the hills, soar towards the church towers, and soar towards the new pavilion. Sixes, fours, every delivery got the treatment. If this went on much longer Kent would not be easily winning and in control but dramatically losing and in disarray. Commonsense and a scoreboard of 97-3 said I had to take myself off. Bowling at the other end was Derek Underwood. Obviously, as our most accurate and experienced bowler, he must continue, that much was clear. But who should take over from me? Bring back Dilley? Bring back Jarvis? Both had bowled so well.

I looked at Kevin Jarvis. He had his sun hat pulled right down over his eyes, indeed so far down you could hardly see his face. But there was no sun. I called to him but in the noise he somehow didn't pick up my voice!

How about a few fast overs?

Yes. I looked at Graham Dilley. But Graham had his back turned to me, talking intently to someone in the crowd!

Well, it's got to be Eldine Baptiste, he'll bowl all day and at anyone. Yes. But Eldine's back seemed to be troubling him, one of those nasty niggling strains, and he gave me a look of pain as I caught his eye. Clearly not fit!

I see. So it's keep going, is it? One more then ...

But one more meant six more, six more balls. Six more balls can mean 36 runs. Six more balls and I could quite easily be in

Above: This picture of Ian Botham shows the same determined look he has whether batting or bowling (*Adrian Murrell*)

Opposite: Six over third man? (*Graham Morris*)

the record books. Remember Gary Sobers at Swansea? The bowler, Malcolm Nash, will never be forgotten. Remember Ian Botham at Taunton, on 14 May 1985, and you of course remember the bowler ... Chris Cowdrey.

The first ball of my next over went for four, which at least meant he could only hit 34 off the over. I asked the umpire how many balls left. Only five? Right, I needed a little variation, I'm always willing to try anything. A slow one was what was required.

It can only go for six and a big Botham six off a slower ball is no more runs in Claude Lewis's scorebook than a small Botham six off a quicker ball.

And it was very slow and it was very wide, and I could sense the umpire on my right wincing. Botham grinned at the sight of the slow, curving ball, and he threw everything at it, teeth bared, moustache bristling, and eyes burning with pleasure.

At this point, with the fielders back-pedalling, I had two pieces of good luck – and I didn't have a lot of luck in 1985. Of the everything Botham threw at my slow, wide delivery only the outside edge of his bat made contact, and, secondly, I had the good fortune to have Alan Knott behind the stumps. Snick.

I. T. Botham, caught Knott, bowled Cowdrey 45.

Somerset 101–4.

Botham? Don't talk to me about Botham, he's no bother!

I looked round. The umpire, pale and relieved, was getting back to his feet. Everyone was running towards me. 'You deserve the Victoria Cross for that delivery.' Jarvis was running towards me, now without his sun hat. Dilley was facing the game. Baptiste seemed to have loosened that pinched nerve. A couple said they quite fancied a bowl, if that was what I and the team required, and what a nice little ground Taunton looked, with the hills and church towers and splendid new pavilion.

(In seriousness, of course, they would all have bowled at Botham.)

At this point the umpire spoke.

'If you bowl another slow half volley like that,' he said, his voice catching with fear, 'if you ever bowl one like that to Ian Botham again, I'll never stand in another Kent match!'

We were comfortable winners and there was only one hurdle to clear before we drove that long M5, M4 journey back. I knew the figure of Mr Botham would be waiting in the pavilion when we walked in. He was. He called me over, he summoned me (and when in Taunton do as you're told!). The dialogue went like this.

I. T. BOTHAM: Cow! Come here!
C. S. COWDREY: Yes, Both.
I. T. BOTHAM: Do you know what you are?
C. S. COWDREY: No, Both. What am I?

I. T. BOTHAM:	You, Cow, are a cafeteria bowler.
C. S. COWDREY:	A cafeteria bowler, Both? What's a cafeteria bowler?
I. T. BOTHAM:	You help yourself to rubbish all along the line, and then at the end you pay for it!

But when all the jokes are over, Ian Botham established in 1985, beyond all doubt, that he is one of the greatest cricketers ever. It is impossible to exaggerate what bowling to him was like. It was just nearly impossible to bowl to him.

On the Taunton ground in 1925 (Jonathan tells me) J. B. Hobbs scored his 126th century to equal Grace's record. On that occasion Percy Fender took him out a bottle and glass. The liquor was reported in the press as champagne and whisky. Hobbs said it was ginger ale. In 1985 Ian Botham deserved whatever drink he called for – if there was any left in Taunton.

(vi)   Kent in 1985: Jonathan Smith

Strange as it must sound, given the appalling summer of 1985, I had full value for my Kent membership card. True, with wipers going, I travelled the M20 and M2 to Canterbury and back three times for nothing more than a glimpse of the cathedral and a sniff of the sewers. But a slow walk round the lovely St Lawrence ground, even in the drizzle, is a fine sight, and at the worst I could buy a few players' badges or photos in the county shop so the children didn't go home empty-handed.

In between the depressions and showers I saw some absorbing cricket. I saw Kent at the bottom, near the top and in the middle. I ran through every emotion every day. Take the Tunbridge Wells week. All right, both matches were defeats, with the wicket doing quite a bit, but they were closely fought and the combination of Courtney Walsh and 'Syd' Lawrence was the most intimidating fast bowling I witnessed. At Tunbridge Wells Kevin Jarvis, as always putting his heart and soul into every delivery, got Tim Robinson lbw 0 first ball, and Robbo's next innings was 170+ in the first Test at Headingley. As so often, Derek Randall was rivetting, the forgotten star of English cricket.

Maidstone week was marvellous. There was sunshine, well,

Over-rate. Now a major talking point in cricket. Here, Gatting,
Hilditch and Gower arrange helmets, thigh pads and shin pads. Where
do we go from here? (*Graham Morris*)

enough to take off your long-sleeve sweater, and we beat Yorkshire and Northants. We hit a purple patch. We were team of the
month in July, winning four out of five, and standing on the bank
at the Mote it was a quiet pleasure seeing Chris Tavaré judge the
pace of the pitch and score so freely, and Eldine Baptiste attack
Roger Harper. Kent looked a top side, which they had not in June
or August. Would 'patchy' be the word?

Claude Lewis. 58 years with Kent,
as player, coach and now as scorer.
A great servant, respected by all of us

I missed Graham Dilley's hat-trick at the Oval, having left one minute earlier to catch a train, but I saw Richard Ellison bowl at Chelmsford. No, don't mention Chelmsford, horror of horrors, that JPL league match on 21 July when we simply had it as good as won with Baptiste and Potter, only to lose. That was the low point of the season for me. I sat with my empty sandwich box in the gloom, a sad figure in a stand full of Essex supporters going on and on about Stuart Turner. How *did* we lose that match! And it was the beginning of our JPL decline.

Behind the stumps Alan Knott was unblemished and perhaps especially at Hesketh Park, Dartford. At Dartford (where we completely outplayed Essex) there was real sunshine and I basked in the sight of Underwood bowling all afternoon, and of Knott keeping and Kent on top, with David Acfield trying to survive while John Lever laughed at the non-striker's end.

Playing golf at Wentworth after the season! (*Hailey Sports Photographic*)

Let's forget the dropped catches and run-outs and overthrows and collapses and if onlys, and remember Simon Hinks's effortless timing, Neil Taylor in top form and so much in control throughout August, and Graham Cowdrey's 50 against the Aussies. Graham got another 50 at Worcester (I was there), a ground which rivals Canterbury, cathedral for cathedral. I did not see Benson's 162 at Southampton, nor my co-author's career best 159 at Canterbury, nor his 131 at Folkestone, nor his two scores of 95 (v Surrey and Middlesex). If Chris had scored five more in those innings would everyone have said: 'He scored four centuries. Good season!'

Above all, it's amusing to recall the *Guardian* cricket writer doubting whether Richard Ellison was 'good enough' to dismiss top order Australians. Well, at Edgbaston, on a good batting wicket, he dismissed Wessels (twice), Border (twice), Wood (once), Phillips (once), McDermott (once) and Holland (twice). In our first outing of an Ashes contest most of us would settle for that middling haul of wickets *and* Man of the Match. Nor was it a flash in the outswinger's pan. Shortly after, at the Oval, Richard did it all over again, and finished top of both the Test and national first-class bowling averages. That achievement was a great thrill for all England, for all Kent and for Tonbridge School people in particular.

Overall, though, Kent were not quite good enough in 1985. Good in patches, good in this or that match, good for a session, but not good enough week in week out to carry off a trophy. When things were close in tight finishes the result tended to go the other way. What would a boring schoolteacher say: 'Could do better'? or 'Should have come higher'?

All the more reason, then, for us fans to look forward to another season.

7

On tour

November 1985. By the log-fire in Jonathan's house. Snow is forecast. Chelsea have just beaten Notts Forest 4–2; Richard Hadlee is tormenting the Australians and Ian Botham is well on his way to Land's End. It's time to reflect on the past season and look forward to another, now only six months away. In those six months England were to travel to the West Indies for a hard tour, and England 'B' to Bangladesh, Sri Lanka and Zimbabwe. By the time you read this we will be into another season. Some of England's 1985 successes may be going through a bad patch, while those who struggled may well now be on a good run. Over a bottle of red wine Jonathan recalled a year ago, when he was leaning over a large world atlas, listening to the Tests in Delhi and Madras. Graeme Fowler had a wonderful series there, yet by the middle of the home season injury and loss of form had forced him not only from the England side, but into the Lancashire 2nd XI. It can happen to any of us. And it does. As usual Foxy (Fowler) looks at the funny side: 'Most people thought when I put my neck out of place I was hanging myself because of my bad run with the bat. In fact it came at a good time. I was on a pair against Malcolm Marshall!'

Malcolm came to Folkestone in September 1985, with a Hampshire team who were making a strong bid for the County Championship. And we had a strange incident. Hampshire made 333 on the first day, a good score on a wicket that looked likely to turn later in the match. The Kent reply was reasonably sound the next morning: at 60–2 there seemed no cause for concern. At this point Mark Benson drove the ball to deep mid-on and set off for an easy single. Rajesh Maru made a vain attempt to stop the ball off his own bowling. With a full-length dive he accidentally collided with Neil Taylor, the non-striker. Neil fell on top of the bowler, and was tussling like a rugby league player trying to be free of his tackler. Meanwhile Benson arrived at the same end ... Marshall had the ball. With Taylor and Maru still locked in a heap, Benson ran a second length of the pitch to be narrowly defeated by a brilliant Caribbean throw to the keeper. Decision: out. Run out. We were amazed that Benson hadn't been called back. This started warfare between Mark Nicholas, the Hampshire captain and his opposite number – me. And I was next man in. Mark explained to me that he had asked the umpires whether he should call Benson back; and the umpires had correctly informed him that they had no option but to give him out. After a brief discussion between Nicholas and Cowdrey on the difference between legality and morality, the battle was on.

Two new captains in 1985. Mark Nicholas of Hampshire tosses the coin. Slight disagreement on the field, but good friends at the end of the day. Mark was appointed captain of England 'B' during our match at Folkestone

Fielding at silly point when Gordon Greenidge is batting can be a
dangerous business! Steve Marsh is the wicketkeeper (*Jack Kay*)

A strange incident, and at the end of the day I don't believe
either captain really knew what was the correct decision. A section
of the Folkestone crowd were certain. As they booed Mark
Nicholas and the Hampshire players off the field at lunch, it was
announced Mark had been appointed captain of the England 'B'
side for the forthcoming tour.

The game was a draw. In our determination not to lose it was
suggested we didn't make a concerted effort to chase a fair target.
Chris Cowdrey, our Boys' Own hero of previous chapters, scored
131, and Hampshire ended up missing out on the title. It was

131 v Hampshire at Folkestone. Bobby Parks is the wicketkeeper. It can't be easy for him to follow Jim (*Ian Stewart*)

disappointing to fall out with the opposition in this way because I enjoy playing against Hampshire; I like to think I get on well with all their players. Yet such is the camaraderie in cricket, I went out to dinner with Mark on the night of the incident. And soon after the season was over we were off to Spain for a holiday together – a much-needed break in that lull between the end of the season and the winter.

Perhaps the most unpredictable period in a cricketer's career is the winter. County players are of course only employed by their clubs for the months April to September. For the rest of the year the majority go abroad to play, usually in Australia or South Africa. Last year out of, say, 340 professionals, I would estimate 180 were wintering overseas. There are few other attractive options open. There aren't many businesses keen to employ someone just for the odd six months. Some cricketers try hard to find work at home but, unqualified for anything, remain unemployed. Some are unwilling to play all year round.

The winter of 1985/6 offered international recognition on two tours, with either England's 'A' or 'B' side. There may well have been fifty or more players quietly hoping for a place either on the demanding West Indies tour or in the B team. Would it be Radella or Kingston? Were the selectors going for one 'top' side and one 'young' side, or would there be a special mix? Excitement, uncertainty, disappointment ... Paul Allott, for example, played in the first four Tests against Australia, yet was left out of both 'A' and 'B' tours. On 1 October 1985 he was looking for a job. Insecurity is the harsh reality, a reality not fully grasped by some supporters.

In the winters of the last decade I have been much more fortunate than most. I have been on twelve tours, playing cricket in about twenty countries. These facts tell you that while I occasionally feel I have experienced the extra pressure of having a famous father, I have even more cause to feel lucky. I first toured as a schoolboy aged 17; then I toured as a young professional of 19 and 20; and I have toured as a (if I may be called one) more 'mature' player. It has been an immense help, and good fun, whatever the tour; a Holmesdale (my Kent League club) tour of Yorkshire, where the emphasis is on survival with the likes of Scott and Cruttenden, or a representative England tour with Gower and Gatting, it doesn't matter.

Touring gives you the chance to adapt to every kind of cricketing demand, every kind of pitch and atmosphere. On tour I have met, played with and played against all kinds, from ex-Test stars to ex-pats. Touring is a concentrated experience when you have to learn to cope with different environments and often considerable travelling and socialising – or in the case of a lot of tours, considerable socialising and some travel. In variable heat, humidity and against opposition of unpredictable quality, team spirit and camaraderie are so important. Above all it is a broadening experience, an eye-opener on the whole cricketing world.

I was still at Tonbridge School when I went on my first overseas tour. It was to South Africa, a first tour and straight in to cricket's most controversial country. The team was called the Crocodiles (why no one can remember) and I captained the side. We left London in a full jumbo on 18 December 1974, and I climbed on board with a row of stitches in my mouth from a rugby injury inflicted two days previously, playing in the last match of the school season. That gives an idea how short of cricket practice the following schoolboys were: C. S. Cowdrey, S. M. Clements, A. K. Cunningham, A. R. Dewes, P. R. Downton, C. J. Evans, D. I. Gower, N. J. Kemp, R. E. P. Lee, I. G. Peck, N. F. M. Popplewell, R. le Q. Savage, C. C. Taylor, R. R. C. Wells, and Managers D. R. Walsh and D. J. Mordaunt.

Our very first practice was spoiled by rain and we struggled badly in the first half of the fixtures against the extraordinarily dedicated and disciplined young South Africans. And when we weren't dealing with their best schoolboys, it was Barry Richards or Kent's Bob Woolmer. It was a demanding, well organised few weeks; Durban, Port Elizabeth, Cape Town, Welkom, Country Clubs and the Vineyard, the Wanderers and Soweto. By the end we had acclimatised and won three and drew two of the last six.

In among the tough lessons there were highlights: two days after we arrived David Gower scored 73 in Durban, making it clear with his timing and natural ability that the Crocodiles had someone special with them. The next day Barry Richards scored 43 and Nick Kemp bowled Bob Woolmer for 0. In Port Elizabeth we watched Graeme Pollock score 120 for Eastern Province (yes, one of those innings which joins the other 'greatest I've ever seen') and we also played against John Waite and Roy McLean. But the tour was most memorable for one reason (other than Paul Downton's legside stumpings). In the African township of Soweto, now sadly familiar on TV news, we were the first overseas side to play against mixed opposition. On matting we faced an African side strengthened by Don Wilson and Barry Stead . . .

However, our main press headline was not Soweto, nor Gower handling gold bars worth a third of a million each, but Downton's views on local girls. When asked whether he liked South African girls Paul innocently said he preferred English ones. The sports pages went to town with a big headline:

'Cowdrey's Crocs don't go for our girls'

Quite what Paul knew about girls from either country I'm sure we'd all like to know, but even at seventeen he and I were beginning to learn the way the press handled comments.

I enjoyed the opportunity of returning to Cape Town for a full season in 1983/4, joining Bob Woolmer at the coloured club Avendale. They were lovely people to play with, and I hope the tremendous effort of Mike Stakol and Bertie Erriksson to promote multiracial cricket won't be wasted or destroyed by the recent troubles.

Gooch and Cowdrey on Muizenburg beach, Cape Town 1983/4. I'm breathing in. Is Graham?!

Having left school in July 1975 I was preparing for my first season in county cricket with Kent. I was working for Leisuresports, who run cricket and golf tours at home and abroad. I was able to go on one of these to Trinidad and Tobago with Hampstead CC. A holiday/club trip to the West Indies is perfect . . . steel bands, rum punches, turquoise water and silver beaches. Then you look down the wicket and see the fast bowlers coming . . . the glossy advertisement clears from your eyes and you try to focus on the ball and your life. But Roger Oakley (tour captain) anticipated the problem and asked 'Young Cowdrey' to 'strengthen the side'.

Yes, well . . . (I was only too pleased).

The first game was on the tip of the tiny island of Tobago at Charlotteville, and the contest had aroused so much interest that a public holiday was announced. Five thousand fans gathered round the country ground to watch a rather jaded Hampstead take on the locals. I was sent in early to get-us-off-to-a-sound-solid-start-sort-of-thing. Yes, of course, I'll do my best.

In my first over I played a perfectly normal forward defensive stroke back down the wicket, only to hear an appeal from cover point. After a moment of intriguing deliberation the umpire gave me out. Out? In disbelief I wandered past the official on my way back to the pavilion. We looked at each other. I found I had to ask him why or indeed how he had given me out. With open enthusiasm he replied:

'You know you weren't out. I know you weren't out. But when your father was here I gave him out too.'

The lads loved it and so did I. It seemed typical of the fun tour and the decision in Charlotteville set the whole flavour of that trip. However after three more games I had only scored three runs and 'the young pro' was keen to make a big score in the final fixture – against Tobago Ladies XI! – but before I got off the mark Gerry Kelly ran me out with cool deliberation. He did me easily with:

'Yes . . . No . . . Yes . . No . . . Wait . . .'

Yes, lovely people to tour with. No, not ideal preparation for the coming Kent season, but wait, there's more to cricket than the county circuit, isn't there?

My next tour of the West Indies was to come sooner than I expected. It was altogether more serious, but hugely enjoyable and successful. I have already made several references to the Young England tour of the West Indies in July–September 1976, but it is worth mentioning here that seven of the party have since played for England, three are county captains and two others have been talked of as possible Test players. We won six of our nine matches including the Test match and One-day International. We drew three. In fact the only disappointment of that 1976 Young England tour was that we only had one Test. On the Trinidad ground. We batted badly in the first innings and only just a little better in the second; while I was pleased to make 48 and 69, with one full day to go our cause looked lost. The West Indies needed only 29 to win with six wickets in hand, and they batted right down the order. Their number 10, for example, had already scored a fine hundred against us. However they panicked and on the final morning our medium pacers, I. Wilks and M. Gatting, ran through them. Great.

The champagne came out around the hotel swimming pool. Fortunately this was paid for by Matthew Pritchard of the Agatha Christie Foundation, a great relief to the Under 19 English cricketers.

There are many fine memories of that tour. A couple of times we came across a young change bowler (he came on fourth

---

Above: M. C. Cowdrey and C. S. Cowdrey as opposition captains. Young England v Old England prior to our tour to the West Indies

Below: Young England touring party to the West Indies 1976. Standing: I. M. Wilks, A. L. Jones, N. J. Kemp, M. K. Fosh, P. J. W. Allott, S. J. Still, D. J. Munden, I. J. Gould, A. S. Patel. Seated: G. H. G. Doggart, D. I. Gower, M. W. Gatting, C. S. Cowdrey, P. R. Downton, R. G. Williams, C. W. J. Athey, L. J. Lenham

change) called Malcolm Marshall; Bill Athey's hundred in Barbados; Mike Gatting's infectious confidence (and his 128 in the One-day International); the effort of Allott, Gould's humour, Gower's brilliance, Downton's support as vice-captain, the terrible trio of Williams, Wilks and Jones ... and of course, what is a tour without An Incident?

In St Kitts I was run out by the bowler while I was backing up. In the West Indies this is called the 'Whitechapel'. The game gradually became very tight 'at the death', with their tail-enders inching closer to our score. With the opposition nine down Mike Gatting, running in to bowl, carried out the second Whitechapel of the match and we were the winners. Two incidents!

It was put to me that we had been rather unsportsmanlike. It was suggested I should have words with Mike Gatting. I agreed to.

'Mike, you must remember we are ambassadors of English cricket, and what you did today ensured we are still unbeaten. Well done!'

I would have been happy to tour West Indies once. However by 1978 I had already been three times; with Hampstead, with Young England, and also to Barbados and Grenada with the League of Gentlemen in early 1977. There was little for me to be proud of in that LOGS tour (batting average 16·5) but then John Newberry averaged 73 with the ball. Make bats, John ... don't bowl at them!

In 1979 I went on a fourth trip to the West Indies, this time with Kent.

Touring with your own county team is something altogether different. By the end of an English season you have all spent six months together: eating, sleeping and talking cricket, winning, losing, travelling up and down motorways, or changing in tiny dressing-rooms. You are 'in each other's pockets' ... And ... Those *socks* ... whose are they? Dilley blames Taylor. Everyone blames Dilley. Playful jokes at Eldine Baptiste's expense ... Jarvo's grunting ... Knotty's kit ... Tav and Dazzler discussing shots ... At least Bob The Mangler (our physio) is listening. No, he's asleep. 'I can't believe it ... it's not raining.' 'What's the plan, Cow?' 'What do you think, Elly?'

After six months of that we usually quite happily go our separate ways. In 1979, however, under the management of Colin Page and Peter Richardson, we set off to see Canada and Antigua. Vancouver is a beautiful place and certainly one I'd like to visit again. In Antigua it poured with rain most of the time, but I'm afraid clearing often enough for us to stop sipping pina coladas and face Andy Roberts and Eldine Baptiste (who we signed soon afterwards). From then on Eldine was on the right side!

I have D. H. Robins to thank for three tours from 1977 to 1980, starting in the Far East. In fact, this one was my first association with Derrick Robins, Chairman of Coventry City FC, formerly on the Warwickshire CCC playing staff and millionaire of Banbury Buildings fame. His greatest love in life (apart from Coventry) is taking teams on tour – at his own expense – to all parts of the world. His selections are strong and likely to overwhelm most opposition. This tour was no exception: M. H. Denness (capt.), M. J. Smith (vice-capt.), P. Carrick, C. S. Cowdrey, J. E. Emburey, D. I. Gower, D. R. Gurr, G. P. Howarth, Intikhab Alam, K. B. S. Jarvis, J. K. Lever, H. Pilling, R. W. Tolchard, P. Willey, J. G. Wright. Manager, J. Lister.

> (JONATHAN: What were you doing in that high-class company?
>
> CHRIS: You may well ask. I felt a bit guilty. Was it my name?)

Cricket tours are full of laughs (Heaven help you if they're not) and with H. Pilling and J. Lever, with John Wright's guitar and Intikhab's solos, this Far East one was among the liveliest. Perhaps *the* liveliest as I was on my third tour with David Gower.

Although the policy was to change room-mates at every port of call, Cowdrey and Gower fixed to stay together most of the way through. We both found silly things very funny, 'sharing a sense of lunacy' as David put it in a later book. Our silliness, if not lunacy, reached its peak in Sri Lanka, the most 'serious' part of the whole tour.

On our first day there it poured and we were stuck in the hotel. It poured. The morning session was no problem: Gower woke at 11.30, Cowdrey 12 noon, but there were still five hours to kill and a siesta seemed unnecessary. By 2 p.m. we had run out of jokes,

duty-free rum and magazines. By 2.15 p.m. I had once again repeated the story of the match between Tonbridge 1st XV v King's,
Canterbury, 1974. I had told the story a hundred times: it was
anyone's game, with minutes to go, as I came into the threequarter
line from fullback, took the ball, and kicked on towards the
opposition line. It was a long chase with their fly-half, both of us
flat out. He had doubled back and was gaining on me all the time.
As we reached their line it was a photo finish, but the ball lay five
yards beyond. His superior pace gave him the edge. We both
dived. He touched the ball just before I did. However, he slid on
the wet ground and I was left holding the ball aloft in a vain
attempt to claim a try ... The referee awarded it and Tonbridge
had taken the lead. The sad picture of the King's fly-half, David
Gower, lying sprawled out near the dead ball line told the story.
You can still see that look of bewilderment when he has been
given a blatantly bad umpiring decision.

During that long, wet Sri Lankan afternoon, with my stories all
over, the cricket bat and ball had to come out. The floor surface
in the hotel room was concrete, firm and true for the occasional
bouncer. I bowled, Gower batted. After an hour of fending the
ball off into chairs or waste bins (my fielders), David's natural
instincts took over and he hooked one into the wall.

Oh dear ... it always ends in tears, doesn't it?

Giggling like schoolboys whose fate is still unknown, we lay on
the bed wondering what to do about the hole in the wall. At this
moment we had an unexpected visitor, an enormous cockroach
the size of a rat. I saw it and sat up. I told Gower to dispose of
it. With the same 2 lb 10 oz bat that had caused the previous
damage he bludgeoned the cockroach into the concrete wicket. It
was an horrific mess. We rang reception to ask for help. Within
seconds a charming Sri Lankan was leaning over the corpse of the
cockroach. He looked up with a sad expression. 'I am very sorry,
sir,' he said to Gower, 'it seems to have died.'

David Gower. Captain of England (*Adrian Murrell*)

We faced the bill for repairs, although D.H.R. helped us out, and we were not allowed to share a room again. Whenever I see David on the balcony of a Test ground, as Man of the Series or successful captain, I think of a bottle of Bollinger, a dead cockroach and a very accurate throwing arm holding a chocolate gateau. But that's another story.

(JONATHAN: But what about the cricket on that tour, real cricket, on *grass*?

CHRIS: Good point. In our next book?)

My second tour with Derrick Robins was in February/March 1979, to South America. To make quite sure we weren't too hard pressed by Chile or Colombia, Derrick Robins lined up the following ... six (later) internationals, led by a superbly funny and eccentric management: C. S. Cowdrey (capt.), C. W. J. Athey, N. E. Briers, R. G. L. Cheatle, I. J. Gould, T. A. Lloyd, D. N. Patel, S. P. Perryman, G. B. Stevenson, L. B. Taylor, K. P. Tomlins, J. P. Whiteley. Managers, P. H. Parfitt, H. Blofeld, Doctor, 'Kelly' Seymour (who played seven times for South Africa).

Once again Derrick Robins was taking us to places I could only have dreamed about, or at least associated with soccer stadiums. Lima in Peru, Buenos Aires and Rio de Janeiro. Will Steve Perryman ever again have 5–0 in Chile? And in Peru Les Taylor must have wondered what was happening as he stood poised to capture the final wicket. Out came the number 11, a young boy with shorts and baseball cap. He faced the daunting task of still requiring 332 for victory. The Leicester paceman had them at 9–9. We gave them a few, to the joy of the spectators but not to the delight of D. H. Robins; D.H.R. wanted them out for less than 10! In Lima it hadn't rained for eleven years, someone said, and I imagined Derek Underwood on the third day....

As captain I was at my least effective in Rio. The 'Test Match' against Brazil was slowly going our way (D. H. Robins XI 330, Brazil 20 and 12–5 overnight). The lads felt they could relax a bit in the New Munich Bar and still clinch victory ... I was unable to find the ground the next morning, and by the time I did the game had been won and lost. First Sri Lanka, then Brazil, and Mr Robins was not amused. But the memories are good: Cheatle in

Lima, Gould in the Hurlingham Club, and Bill Athey proving in Buenos Aires that you can get runs without sleep.

My final tour with D.H.R. was to Australasia. This time we faced our stiffest opposition of all his tours. But again it was a strong side: C. S. Cowdrey (capt.), C. W. J. Athey (vice-capt.), K. J. Barnett, N. G. B. Cook, K. E. Cooper, A. L. Jones, C. Maynard, W. G. Merry, G. J. Parsons, D. N. Patel, A. C. S. Pigott, C. J. Richards, K. Sharp, G. C. Small, R. G. Williams. Manager, B. E. Simmons.

Given the quality, we didn't play to the best of our ability. Certainly as captain I got off to an indifferent start. At our first practice on a school ground I had been given a team sheet of all tour players, explaining exactly what each did. Of course I knew the majority but there were one or two I hadn't come across before.

Gordon Parsons of Leicestershire was one. He was listed as a top order batsman and occasional bowler. As I know now that was a mistake. Although Gordon has made the odd good score for Leicester, he is a bowler. However, he seemed fairly quiet so I thought I would give him a bat early, straight after Athey and Sharp. Before Gordon's turn to bat came he had to field for a short while to make up the numbers, and I thought it rather strange he should be wearing such enormous bowling boots to field at first slip. Surely he wasn't going to bat in them as well? He did. He struggled against the pace of Pigott and Small. He was dismissed and hit a number of times.

After his knock he returned to first slip in his bowling boots. Eventually, at the end of the day, I had a bat. While batting I remembered Gordon was down as an 'occasional bowler' so I asked him to have a few overs. He paced out a very long run. He roared in from the sight screen. Bouncers, everything. I wasn't amused. My partner and I slogged him, not believing he was a bowler at all.

I was even less amused when I realised what a bad mistake I'd made: to put a bowler in early to face our two fastest bowlers, and then to slog him when he was rusty, having had no practice all winter ... I had not displayed great leadership quality. Poor old Gordon.

During the tour I came in for some more criticism, this time from Kim Barnett. I've been called a lot of things, but not negative. In what way had I been negative? Wasn't it obvious, Kim said, I hadn't bowled his leg spinners on the first two days of our match against Young New Zealand. All right, so on the third I bowled Kim and reminded myself why I hadn't bowled him on the first two. Despite the hammering he took, Kim still asked me to be best man at his wedding to Nancy in 1984 – a very pleasant duty and one which came to me from touring.

Touring gives you a chance to meet players from other counties, some players you might never get to know any other way. Not everyone, though, has been so appreciative of my contribution. The final blow of the D. H. Robins Australasia tour was at Heathrow. As we walked down from the plane Nick Cook came over to me and said:

'Well, Cow, it's been a great experience playing under your captaincy. But not a good one.'

The Australia section of that D.H.R. tour was a very brief one (much of the time we were in New Zealand), but it was one of the four visits I've had there. Just after Christmas in 1977 I was leaving home for Sydney, my first cricketing venture in Australia. With John Emburey, John Hopkins and Jim Love, I had won a Whitbread Scholarship. Sydney is as lovely a city as you'll find, and the cricket rather more competitive than our Far East tour! It took me some time to come to terms with playing only once a week, and normally only batting once a fortnight. There is enormous pressure to bat well each time: from an overseas player much is expected, and I went to the crease six or seven times where I would have batted thirty times or more in England.

Unfortunately my club in 1977/8 (Cumberland, in Parramatta) was not a particularly strong side and I always hoped I would rejoin them for a full winter. This I did in 1982/3. This time, though, Jon Agnew of Leicestershire and England came with me. Jim Love was again out in Sydney and we shared a flat in Neutral Bay. (A Yorkshireman and Kentishman *can* get on, you see.)

Our captain in Parramatta was John Benaud (Richie's brother), a very likeable extrovert who missed a large section of the season after being struck in the cheekbone on a wet wicket.

I was honoured to be asked to captain Cumberland and I immediately put my theory into practice: insert the opposition every game (unheard-of in Sydney Grade cricket) in the hope Cumberland could win a few 'outright'. To an Englishman their competition has a strange format: the main contest is over two Saturdays and is decided on the first innings. The winners collect six points. However, should you succeed in bowling the opposition out twice you then collect an 'outright' ten points. We had ground to make up in the league table so I banked on fortune favouring the brave. 'Outright it is.'

We won the next four, then discovered why it wasn't such a good idea to bowl first every time. Away from home a new pattern emerged. We would bowl the opposition out for around 200 and be well placed at 70-1 on a good wicket. When we returned to the opposition ground next week, however, things looked different. A touch of green had tinged the wicket, the groundsman hadn't been able to cut the outfield ... and ... a probable victory turned into a simple defeat.

Oh, well ... We were learning all the time, and the friends we made were there to greet us in 1985 when we toured with England.

In amongst all these ventures there was one more unusual trip. Playing for E. W. Swanton's XI, the Arabs, I went to Kenya. We are not now dealing with the odd 'son of', for the family connections on this tour were numerous. Charlie Fry is the grandson of C. B. Fry, and Mark Faber the grandson of Harold Macmillan. Simon Doggart's father Hubert (manager of the Young England tour of the West Indies in 1976) holds the record of scoring a double century on his first-class debut for Cambridge v Lancashire. Alistair Peebles is the son of Ian Peebles, whose history goes too far back for me! Jim Swanton was staggered when I told him I was a bit vague on the career of Ian Peebles.

E.W.S: You don't know Ian Peebles. Good God! What an extraordinary thing! You've got some learning to do, my boy ... In the 1930 Ashes series – Don Bradman had scored a hundred in the first Test, two hundred in the second Test, three hundred in the third, and the bookies weren't even accepting bets on a Bradman four hundred in the fourth, when he was caught – no, not for 400, but for only 14 off Ian Peebles' leg spin.

C.S.C: Yes, Jim.

Apart from my bowling it was a fun tour, and an honour to play with Conrad Hunte.

E.W.S: Conrad Cleophas Hunte, 44 Tests, vice-captain to Garfield Sobers, a century on his Test debut, one of the most reliable West Indian opening batsmen there's ever been, averaging 45·06 – and of course a delightful person, a privilege to play with or against.

C.S.C: Yes, Jim.

As a record of the places where I've used a cricket bat I must include Corfu, La Manga, Scotland and Wales (v Glamorgan). In La Manga there was a pro-celebrity competition. In the cricket section I partnered Phil Edmonds, who inflicted serious damage on the comedian Lenny Bennett. He hit a lofted shot to long-on, to the very spot Lenny was fielding. Misjudgment and mouth open, Lenny lost eleven teeth. There was a feeling this would stop him talking. It didn't.

In Scotland Kent went on a tour to Fochabers (say that when you've had a few).

I haven't listed all these tours to appear self-satisfied but to show the extent of my travels. From Auckland to Vancouver, from Argentina to Mombassa, I've toured – and I've been the lucky person who has benefited from other people's organisation and generosity, Jim Swanton's, Derrick Robins' and many others'.

The good memories of all the players I've mentioned, and many that I haven't: Dudley Owen-Thomas eating wine glasses in Nairobi; Geoff Howarth naming me 'Claret'; losing my clothes in Rio; and Bill Merry playing 'jacks' in up-country New Zealand.

Touring is a tremendous thrill, provided you keep your feet on the ground. Varying climates, monsoons and heatwaves, kindness, sunshine and silliness, the experience is unparalleled and the fun I've had is beyond my ability to describe. Without doubt the pinnacle for me was the tour with England in India 1984/5. But at its most serious level touring can be hard. There can be a price to pay. . . .

England touring party to India and Australia 1984/5.
Standing: G. Fowler, V. J. Marks, P. R. Downton, M. D. Moxon, R. M. Ellison, N. A. Foster, N. G. Cowans, C. S. Cowdrey, R. T. Robinson, B. N. French, G. G. A. Saulez.
Seated: B. W. Thomas, A. J. Lamb, P. I. Pocock, M. W. Gatting, D. I. Gower, A. S. Brown, P. H. Edmonds, P. J. W. Allott, N. Gifford

Cricket, cricket, cricket.

Christmas, and at the biggest family occasion of the year the Cowdreys very rarely had everyone there. By chance Christmas Eve is also M. C. Cowdrey's birthday, so he was never there for his birthday either. He couldn't be. For fourteen years he was on tour with England, but on four occasions he didn't leave until the New Year. Four years out of eighteen.

Family practice: Jeremy in the gully, Mum at 2nd slip, Carol at 1st slip, Dad coaching, Graham batting, and my first experience at short-leg (*Keystone*)

These long trips put a terrible strain on family life and any marriage. For many years the wives were not expected to join cricket tours, and to be at home for such lengthy periods with young children was not easy. Perhaps the strain would be less if the player could rest at home for six weeks or so afterwards, but in cricket it rarely happens. The season starts. Off you go again ... hotels, away from home. Certainly things have improved: travelling is quicker, family arrangements more civilised and tours shorter, but some strains have increased with seven-day-a-week cricket.

Cricket, cricket, cricket.

My sister Carolyn must have wondered whether we realised she was in the Cowdrey family at all. 'Dad's home for lunch.' 'Oh good.' And three hours later Colin, Chris, Jeremy and Graham would be on the fourth day's play on the third Test at Brisbane or Kingston or Karachi. Three boys and a mother who had to like cricket (and does) would listen and go on all day asking,

'What's Gary Sobers like?'

'Is Bobby Simpson nice?'

And so on.

Poor Carol. When she mentioned riding or netball she realised it wasn't down on the agenda. Riding? Netball? But Carol has come through it all very well and now does enough of her own talking!

What about Jeremy, next son down?

Jeremy's problems were slightly different. He plays every sport well, without being outstanding at any, yet everyone expected him to shine at cricket. Three years in the Tonbridge School 1st XI is 'good enough', even excellent, but he knew only too well what was 'expected'. Jeremy loves a day out at the weekend to play club games, a couple of pints, a quick 20, a wicket or two at reasonable cost with his leg breaks, and back to the friendly social life with the opposition. It isn't a lot to ask.

For a while though Jay gave it all up. For too many people he was Saturday's centre of attraction. 'I wonder how good *this* Cowdrey is.' Jeremy didn't care how good a cricketer he was – he wanted to enjoy his day. Cricket, cricket, cricket – stuff your cricket? Yet he is an avid follower and a great ally, an open ear whenever I need to talk to someone, and I hope he'll still talk to me after seeing the photo overleaf.

Also in the photograph, at slip, is my youngest brother, Graham. As is the case with all current Kent players, I don't want to say too much about Graham, who is not only brilliant at every sport but he was also a hard worker in class ... we accepted him into the family eventually! I hope he will be a top cricketer: his natural ability, determination and positive attitude suggest he could be.

In the winter of 1985/6 he toured India with 'Christians in Sport'. Under the guidance of Vic Marks and Andrew

Wingfield-Digby he impressed with a century and some accomplished fifties. A year after I'd been there Graham, too, played in Bangalore, Madras and Hyderabad, in a style which Vic described as 'less classical than his father, but more orthodox than his brother: he surely has a rosy future in the game – if he can cope with his surname.' Remembering 1984/5, Vic expected hundreds of people wanting to meet another 'Son of Colin', hundreds ready to tell Graham: 'I knew your father.' Graham expected the same. But no! All he received was 'I knew your brother Chris.' That amused me for weeks.

Tonbridge School: the Head. Brother Jeremy has just bowled a wide. Is he about to show dissent? Graham is at first slip (*Martin King*)

Jeremy has been most helpful and Graham is a team-mate, but there's no doubt at all who my greatest supporter has been. I'll never forget being out first ball in Melbourne, a 'disaster', but more importantly I remember that night because my mother rang me from England to say 'Bad luck!' It sounds simple, even a corny thing to do, but she said: 'I would have rung you if you had done particularly well, so I wanted to ring anyway.'

Through rain or shine she'll come to watch Kent, praying I'll do well, yet philosophical about whatever the day brings. There's always tomorrow. This is not an easy position, especially with the intense disappointment of sportsmen, yet my mother has supported all the family with remarkable vigour; she has supported us in the best possible way, quietly and modestly, never wanting or expecting the limelight.

Cricket, cricket, cricket.

He was destined to play, I suppose. Once his father had given him the initials MCC it was on the cards. Perhaps if MCC had given me CFC I might have played for Chelsea? Still, CSC could be Chelsea Supporters Club?

Michael Colin Cowdrey, the way he timed the ball! Finding 'big' photos of Ian Botham's strokes is easy; finding photos of my father playing exciting shots is difficult simply because they often look like defensive strokes, yet so fine was his timing the ball sped off his bat. I remember him spending time with me in the Tonbridge School racquets court, trying to help me with my off-side play. He was amazed I should find it so difficult to hit a length ball just outside off stumps through the covers for four.

'It's a knack,' he used to say. 'Once you've got it you'll never lose it.'

He reckoned that once he had become accustomed to a certain bowler he would pick out an advertising board in between cover and extra and aim for it. The irritating thing was he expected to hit the board! Although always calm and controlled when batting, he was (I'm told) lacking in confidence. I'll never forget Peter Richardson's words: 'I wonder how good he would have been if he had believed in himself.' Well, confident or not, he was certainly good enough!

My father never tried to talk me into playing cricket. I admire and thank him for that. Of course, like all fathers of sports-mad

Above: One-day International at Bangalore. It doesn't look like it, but I was disappointed to be 12th man in my father's birthplace (*Graham Morris*)

Opposite: A break in the One-day International in Bangalore. As bottles were being thrown on to the pitch, Gavaskar led his team off the field. Downton and Lamb are now trying to get the 12th man (me) to bring them a drink (*Adrian Murrell*)

sons, he threw me ball after ball in the garden, but he encouraged me to play all games and never once brought up the subject of a professional career until I had been offered my first Kent contract in 1976. He would have loved to play a match with me, but apart from the fact that one-day cricket was becoming a strain for him, he knew only too well his presence in the same side would have added to the pressure on me. (Could we have been fighting for the same place?) Ironically, with Kent suffering from injuries and Test calls, and with C. S. Cowdrey, P. R. Downton and N. J. Kemp on tour in the West Indies, M. C. Cowdrey was recalled to play one match against Surrey at Canterbury. So, in my first season on the Kent staff, my father played and I didn't!

If that strange stroke of fate was his disappointment, mine was in India with the England team. There I met friends of the family and saw E. A. Cowdrey's (his father's) name on the club board in Madras. And when we visited Bangalore, my father's birthplace, I was for special, sentimental reasons, keen to play in the One-Day International.

In the nets the day before the match, Richard Ellison, remembering I had bowled him a bouncer in the nets at Bombay, repaid the compliment. Not expecting it, I played the ball very badly and was struck on the arm. For a while it looked as if it might be broken. I was upset at the possibility of not being available for selection, but an ice-pack and Bernard Thomas confirmed hypochondria. I was passed fit, but still made 12th man. A major disappointment.

I am sorry I didn't see my father more when I was a child, and even more that the strain on their marriage told. My father and my mother have been through a lot. I hope they will both find happiness. They deserve it.

8

Flashback

Before Chris and I started to write this book I realised that although I had known him well since he was thirteen years old, I had very little idea of his earlier years. Of course he had things he wanted to say about his prep school Wellesley House – his first experiences of competitive sport and his growing awareness of his father's famous name – but what did those at Wellesley think of Chris? What was it like having 'Son of' in the school?

I wrote to Bill Sale, the Headmaster, and asked for his opinion of C. S. Cowdrey between the ages of eight and thirteen. This is what he sent me.

Christopher Cowdrey
at Wellesley House 1965–70

Christopher Cowdrey came to Wellesley House in 1965 on the recommendation of his grandfather, Stuart Chiesman, who had often come to the school to watch Kent 2nd XI games which used to be played there.

The spotlight was on him from the beginning. The first decision was whether the TV cameras should be allowed to take Christopher arriving with his parents for his first day. It was decided not to let in the cameramen and this policy was pursued throughout his time at the school.

On the occasion when Colin was playing in his 100th Test Match at Edgbaston, Penny was wicketkeeping for the Mothers v the Boys (as she did for many years) and Christopher was playing for the School's 1st XI, the BBC were naturally anxious to record the triple event. Fortunately they were sympathetic to the school's view that Christopher should not be singled out at this stage of his life on account of his father's fame. Of course he was, and greatly to the School's advantage. His father on several occasions gave batting demonstrations in the nets and he took fielding practices with the 1st XI. A Kent cricketer usually accompanied him on these occasions and as a result Christopher became a hero to the other boys.

However, he soon earned his own recognition as a cricketer of outstanding talent. Duncan Fraser, the Housemaster of the house where boys went for their first year, used to bring Christopher up to Wellesley to play with the Colts as he was too good for his own age group. In his first summer at the school, aged 8, Christopher scored 50 and took 5 wickets in his first appearance in a school match, against Stone House. Initially our opponents had wondered why such a young boy had been included in the team, but Christopher's contribution quickly silenced the doubters.

After such a spectacular start, probably too much was expected of him but this is the lot of a son with a famous father. There is no doubt that this affected Christopher. Very naturally he felt overawed at times; also not surprisingly he sometimes took advantage of his special position. The point was it was impossible for him to be 'normal', and indeed he isn't normal. Quite apart from the special position he found himself in due to his father's fame, Christopher is a very positive personality, in many ways more positive than his father, and he is an exceptional cricketer in his own right; his most impressive record at the school conclusively proves this point.

He was a lucky batsman: frequently it seemed he had a lucky 'let off' at an early stage in an innings, but his instinct was to attack the bowling and luck often favours the brave in cricket. He also had obvious flaws in his technique: his forward defensive shot was by no means a model, in spite of much patient instruction. He relied heavily on his great natural ability and it was inevitable that at some stage his technical frailties would be found out when he played a higher standard of cricket. At this stage he didn't appear particularly interested in batting technique, probably because he found it so easy to make runs with the method he had, he saw no reason to change it. He loved playing in the nets but he

Early coaching from the 'Old Man' . . .

. . . and Sir Garfield Sobers

was not a meticulous practiser. He enjoyed hitting a cricket ball
and bowling people out. This was how he played his cricket as he
was a natural competitor. He would bowl or bat as the situation
required and he was not much concerned with style.

Even at Wellesley it was obvious that he was a notably unselfish
cricketer. Always, he played willingly for his side, but perhaps his
greatest contribution was his fielding and his enthusiasm which
affected all those around him. This gift for infectious leadership
often turned a match which seemed a lost cause into an unexpected victory. The most spectacular example was the occasion
when Wellesley were bowled out for 29 and, largely through
Christopher's bowling and his will to win, St Lawrence Junior
School were bowled out for 27!

As a boy Christopher was always likeable and he was deservedly
popular as he was exceedingly modest and always prepared to
encourage others far less talented than himself. He was also mis-
chievous and would get away with what he could, especially on
the work front, but he was never dishonest or sly. He had a
cheerful disregard for authority but he was seldom deliberately
obstructive. He tried to avoid getting caught, but if he was he
took what was coming and reckoned the risk had been worth
taking.

When Christopher left to go to Tonbridge he was developing a
slightly reckless adolescent streak which we hoped would be tempered by his naturally kind nature and his genuine sensitivity
towards other people's feelings.

No one doubted his ability as a cricketer but doubts were ex-
pressed about his technique and it was hoped that he would listen
to advice and 'straighten up' before it was too late, if his ambition
was to be a professional cricketer, as it clearly was. This was
particularly important as in the classroom he had only just done
enough to satisfy the Tonbridge examiners.

Christopher was fun to have around. As his headmaster, I found
him exciting to teach as a cricketer, but I needed 'eyes in the back
of my head' to know all that he was up to. However, he had a
winning way with people of all ages and he was naturally cour-
teous. We felt that provided at some stage he put personal discipline higher on his list of priorities, he had the ingredients to be a
great cricketer and certainly a great captain.

W. F. Sale

JONATHAN:	That's good.
CHRIS:	What do you mean 'That's good'?
JONATHAN:	Well, it's very complimentary.
CHRIS:	He calls me a lucky batsman … with obvious flaws in my technique.
JONATHAN:	Well?
CHRIS:	Not a meticulous practiser …
JONATHAN:	Well?
CHRIS:	Stop saying well, will you?
JONATHAN:	But he's a good friend of yours, isn't he?
CHRIS:	Yes.
JONATHAN:	Well …
CHRIS:	You're doing it again!
JONATHAN:	Sorry.
CHRIS:	Yes, he's a nice guy, Bill.
JONATHAN:	So, what's the problem?
CHRIS:	He says I had a cheerful disregard for authority.
JONATHAN:	Seldom deliberately obstructive though.
CHRIS:	A reckless adolescent streak.
JONATHAN:	With a kind nature though.
CHRIS:	Lack of personal discipline – what's he on about?
JONATHAN:	Don't you like what he says?
CHRIS:	No.
JONATHAN:	Why not?
CHRIS:	It's all true.
JONATHAN:	Exactly.